Dotty for Diamonds

● ◇ ● ◇ ● ◇ ● ◇ ● ◇ ●

NAME OF
DESIGN:

CANVAS SIZE: _____
PICTURE SIZE: _____
SQUARE DRILL ☐   ROUND DRILL ○

I PURCHASED THIS KIT FROM:
(OR IT WAS GIFTED BY)

_____
PRICE: [_____]

DATE STARTED: / / /
DATE OF
COMPLETION: / / /

ADVANCED
INTERMEDIATE
BEGINNER

HOW MUCH I LOVED
THIS PROJECT ♡
◇ ◇ ◇ ◇ ◇

AFTER THE COMPLETION OF THIS PIECE I:

KEPT IT FOR MYSELF ◇   SOLD IT ◇

GIFTED IT TO A LOVED ONE ◇   OTHER ◇

I GIFTED IT TO: _____
OR I SOLD IT FOR [_____] ON/AT _____
_____ ON THE / / /

NOTES & IDEAS FOR THE NEXT PROJECT:

_____
_____
_____
_____

stick picture here

◇•◇•◇•◇•◇•◇•◇•◇•◇•◇•◇•◇•◇•◇•◇•◇

NAME OF
DESIGN:

CANVAS SIZE: _____

PICTURE SIZE: _____

SQUARE DRILL ☐   ROUND DRILL ○

DATE STARTED: / / /

DATE OF
COMPLETION: / / /

I PURCHASED THIS KIT FROM:
(OR IT WAS GIFTED BY)

_____

PRICE: [   ]

ADVANCED

INTERMEDIATE

BEGINNER

HOW MUCH I LOVED
THIS PROJECT ♡

◇ ◇ ◇ ◇ ◇

AFTER THE COMPLETION OF THIS PIECE I:

KEPT IT FOR MYSELF ◇   SOLD IT ◇

GIFTED IT TO A LOVED ONE ◇   OTHER ◇

I GIFTED IT TO:_____

OR I SOLD IT FOR [   ] ON/AT_____

_____ ON THE / / /

NOTES & IDEAS FOR THE NEXT PROJECT:

_____
_____
_____
_____
_____

◇·◇·◇·◇·◇·◇·◇·◇·◇·◇·◇·◇·◇·◇·◇·◇·◇

stick picture here

NAME OF
DESIGN:

CANVAS SIZE: _____

PICTURE SIZE: _____

SQUARE DRILL ☐   ROUND DRILL ○

DATE STARTED: / /

DATE OF
COMPLETION: / /

I PURCHASED THIS KIT FROM:
(OR IT WAS GIFTED BY)

ADVANCED

INTERMEDIATE

BEGINNER

HOW MUCH I LOVED
THIS PROJECT ♡

◇ ◇ ◇ ◇ ◇

_____

PRICE: [   ]

AFTER THE COMPLETION OF THIS PIECE I:

KEPT IT FOR MYSELF ◇   SOLD IT ◇

GIFTED IT TO A LOVED ONE ◇   OTHER ◇

I GIFTED IT TO: _____

OR I SOLD IT FOR [   ] ON/AT _____

_____   ON THE / /

NOTES & IDEAS FOR THE NEXT PROJECT:

_____

_____

_____

_____

stick picture here

◇·◇·◇·◇· ◇·◇·◇·◇·◇·◇·◇·◇·◇·◇·◇·◇·◇·◇·◇·◇

NAME OF
DESIGN:

CANVAS SIZE: _____

PICTURE SIZE: _____

SQUARE DRILL ☐   ROUND DRILL ○

I PURCHASED THIS KIT FROM:
(OR IT WAS GIFTED BY)

_____

PRICE: [   ]

AFTER THE COMPLETION OF THIS PIECE I:

KEPT IT FOR MYSELF ◇   SOLD IT ◇

GIFTED IT TO A LOVED ONE ◇   OTHER ◇

I GIFTED IT TO: _____

OR I SOLD IT FOR [   ] ON/AT _____

_____ ON THE / / /

NOTES & IDEAS FOR THE NEXT PROJECT:

_____

_____

_____

_____

_____

◇·◇·◇·◇·◇·◇·◇·◇·◇·◇·◇·◇·◇·◇·◇·◇·◇

DATE STARTED: / / /

DATE OF
COMPLETION: / / /

ADVANCED

INTERMEDIATE

BEGINNER

HOW MUCH I LOVED
THIS PROJECT ♡

◇ ◇ ◇ ◇ ◇

stick picture here

NAME OF
DESIGN:

CANVAS SIZE: _____

PICTURE SIZE: _____

SQUARE DRILL ☐   ROUND DRILL ○

I PURCHASED THIS KIT FROM:
(OR IT WAS GIFTED BY)

_____

PRICE: [   ]

AFTER THE COMPLETION OF THIS PIECE I:

KEPT IT FOR MYSELF ◇   SOLD IT ◇

GIFTED IT TO A LOVED ONE ◇   OTHER ◇

I GIFTED IT TO:_____

OR I SOLD IT FOR [   ] ON/AT_____

_____ ON THE / /

NOTES & IDEAS FOR THE NEXT PROJECT:

_____

_____

_____

_____

DATE STARTED: / /
DATE OF
COMPLETION: / /

ADVANCED
INTERMEDIATE
BEGINNER

HOW MUCH I LOVED
THIS PROJECT ♡

◇ ◇ ◇ ◇ ◇

stick picture here

◇·◇·◇·◇·◇·◇·◇·◇·◇·◇·◇·◇·◇·◇·◇·◇·◇

NAME OF
DESIGN:

CANVAS SIZE: _____

PICTURE SIZE: _____

SQUARE DRILL ☐   ROUND DRILL ○

DATE STARTED: / / /

DATE OF
COMPLETION: / / /

I PURCHASED THIS KIT FROM:
(OR IT WAS GIFTED BY)

ADVANCED

INTERMEDIATE

BEGINNER

HOW MUCH I LOVED
THIS PROJECT ♡

◇ ◇ ◇ ◇ ◇

_____

PRICE: [   ]

AFTER THE COMPLETION OF THIS PIECE I:

KEPT IT FOR MYSELF ◇   SOLD IT ◇

GIFTED IT TO A LOVED ONE ◇   OTHER ◇

I GIFTED IT TO: _____

OR I SOLD IT FOR [   ] ON/AT _____

_____ ON THE / / /

NOTES & IDEAS FOR THE NEXT PROJECT:

_____
_____
_____
_____
_____

◇·◇·◇·◇·◇·◇·◇·◇·◇·◇·◇·◇·◇·◇·◇·◇

stick picture here

Name of
design:

Canvas size: _____

picture size: _____

Square drill ☐   Round drill ○

I purchased this kit from:
(or it was gifted by)

_____

Price: [_____]

After the completion of this piece I:

Kept it for myself ◇   Sold it ◇

Gifted it to a loved one ◇   Other ◇

I gifted it to: _____

or I sold it for [_____] on/at _____

_____ on the / / /

Notes & ideas for the next project:

_____
_____
_____
_____
_____

Date started: / / /

Date of
completion: / / /

How much I loved
this project ♡

◇ ◇ ◇ ◇ ◇

Advanced

Intermediate

Beginner

stick picture here

◇·◇·◇·◇·◇·◇·◇·◇·◇·◇·◇·◇·◇·◇·◇·◇·◇·◇·◇·◇

NAME OF
DESIGN:

CANVAS SIZE: _____

PICTURE SIZE: _____

SQUARE DRILL ☐   ROUND DRILL ○

DATE STARTED: / / /

DATE OF
COMPLETION: / / /

I PURCHASED THIS KIT FROM:
(OR IT WAS GIFTED BY)

_____

PRICE: [   ]

ADVANCED

INTERMEDIATE

BEGINNER

HOW MUCH I LOVED
THIS PROJECT ♡

◇ ◇ ◇ ◇ ◇

AFTER THE COMPLETION OF THIS PIECE I:

KEPT IT FOR MYSELF ◇   SOLD IT ◇

GIFTED IT TO A LOVED ONE ◇   OTHER ◇

I GIFTED IT TO:_____

OR I SOLD IT FOR [   ] ON/AT_____

_____ ON THE / / /

NOTES & IDEAS FOR THE NEXT PROJECT:

_____

_____

_____

_____

_____

◇·◇·◇·◇·◇·◇·◇·◇·◇·◇·◇·◇·◇·◇·◇·◇·◇·◇·◇·◇

stick picture here

NAME OF
DESIGN:

CANVAS SIZE: _____

PICTURE SIZE: _____

SQUARE DRILL ☐   ROUND DRILL ○

I PURCHASED THIS KIT FROM:
(OR IT WAS GIFTED BY)

_____

PRICE: [_____]

ADVANCED
INTERMEDIATE
BEGINNER

DATE STARTED: / /

DATE OF
COMPLETION: / /

HOW MUCH I LOVED
THIS PROJECT ♡
◇ ◇ ◇ ◇ ◇

AFTER THE COMPLETION OF THIS PIECE I:

KEPT IT FOR MYSELF ◇   SOLD IT ◇

GIFTED IT TO A LOVED ONE ◇   OTHER ◇

I GIFTED IT TO:_____
OR I SOLD IT FOR [_____] ON/AT_____
_____ ON THE / /

NOTES & IDEAS FOR THE NEXT PROJECT:

_____
_____
_____
_____

stick picture here

◇·◇·◇·◇·◇·◇·◇·◇·◇·◇·◇·◇·◇·◇·◇·◇·◇·◇

NAME OF
DESIGN:

CANVAS SIZE: _____

PICTURE SIZE: _____

SQUARE DRILL ☐   ROUND DRILL ○

DATE STARTED: / / /

DATE OF
COMPLETION: / / /

I PURCHASED THIS KIT FROM:
(OR IT WAS GIFTED BY)

ADVANCED

INTERMEDIATE

BEGINNER

HOW MUCH I LOVED
THIS PROJECT ♡

◇ ◇ ◇ ◇ ◇

_____

PRICE: [   ]

AFTER THE COMPLETION OF THIS PIECE I:

KEPT IT FOR MYSELF ◇   SOLD IT ◇

GIFTED IT TO A LOVED ONE ◇   OTHER ◇

I GIFTED IT TO: _____

OR I SOLD IT FOR [   ] ON/AT _____

_____ ON THE / / /

NOTES & IDEAS FOR THE NEXT PROJECT:

_____

_____

_____

_____

_____

stick picture here

◇·◇·◇·◇·◇·◇·◇·◇·◇·◇·◇·◇·◇·◇·◇·◇·◇◇◇

NAME OF
DESIGN:

CANVAS SIZE: _____

PICTURE SIZE: _____

SQUARE DRILL ☐   ROUND DRILL ○

I PURCHASED THIS KIT FROM:
(OR IT WAS GIFTED BY)

_____

PRICE: [_____]

AFTER THE COMPLETION OF THIS PIECE I:

KEPT IT FOR MYSELF ◇   SOLD IT ◇

GIFTED IT TO A LOVED ONE ◇   OTHER ◇

I GIFTED IT TO: _____
OR I SOLD IT FOR [_____] ON/AT _____

_____ ON THE / / /

NOTES & IDEAS FOR THE NEXT PROJECT:

_____

_____

_____

_____

DATE STARTED: / / /
DATE OF
COMPLETION: / / /

ADVANCED
INTERMEDIATE
BEGINNER

HOW MUCH I LOVED
THIS PROJECT ♡
◇ ◇ ◇ ◇ ◇

stick picture here

◇•◇•◇•◇•◇•◇•◇•◇•◇•◇•◇•◇•◇•◇•◇•◇•◇•◇◇

NAME OF
DESIGN:

CANVAS SIZE: _____

PICTURE SIZE: _____

SQUARE DRILL ☐   ROUND DRILL ○

I PURCHASED THIS KIT FROM:
(OR IT WAS GIFTED BY)

_____

PRICE: [_____]

DATE STARTED: / / /

DATE OF
COMPLETION: / / /

ADVANCED
INTERMEDIATE
BEGINNER

HOW MUCH I LOVED
THIS PROJECT ♡

◇ ◇ ◇ ◇ ◇

AFTER THE COMPLETION OF THIS PIECE I:

KEPT IT FOR MYSELF ◇   SOLD IT ◇

GIFTED IT TO A LOVED ONE ◇   OTHER ◇

I GIFTED IT TO:_____

OR I SOLD IT FOR [_____] ON/AT _____

_____   ON THE / / /

NOTES & IDEAS FOR THE NEXT PROJECT:

_____

_____

_____

_____

stick picture here

◇◇◇◇◇◇◇◇◇◇◇◇◇◇◇◇◇◇◇◇◇◇

NAME OF
DESIGN:

CANVAS SIZE: _____

PICTURE SIZE: _____

SQUARE DRILL ☐   ROUND DRILL ○

I PURCHASED THIS KIT FROM:
(OR IT WAS GIFTED BY)

_____

PRICE: [   ]

ADVANCED
INTERMEDIATE
BEGINNER

DATE STARTED: / / /
DATE OF
COMPLETION: / / /

HOW MUCH I LOVED
THIS PROJECT ♡

◇ ◇ ◇ ◇ ◇

AFTER THE COMPLETION OF THIS PIECE I:

KEPT IT FOR MYSELF ◇   SOLD IT ◇

GIFTED IT TO A LOVED ONE ◇   OTHER ◇

I GIFTED IT TO:_____
OR I SOLD IT FOR [   ] ON/AT_____
_____ ON THE / / /

NOTES & IDEAS FOR THE NEXT PROJECT:

_____

_____

_____

_____

stick picture here

◇•◇•◇•◇•◇•◇•◇•◇•◇•◇•◇•◇•◇•◇•◇•◇

NAME OF
DESIGN:

CANVAS SIZE: _____

PICTURE SIZE: _____

SQUARE DRILL ☐   ROUND DRILL ○

I PURCHASED THIS KIT FROM:
(OR IT WAS GIFTED BY)

_____

PRICE: ☐

AFTER THE COMPLETION OF THIS PIECE I:

KEPT IT FOR MYSELF ◇   SOLD IT ◇

GIFTED IT TO A LOVED ONE ◇   OTHER ◇

I GIFTED IT TO: _____

OR I SOLD IT FOR ☐ ON/AT _____

_____ ON THE / /

NOTES & IDEAS FOR THE NEXT PROJECT:

_____
_____
_____
_____
_____

◇·◇·◇·◇·◇·◇·◇·◇·◇·◇·◇·◇·◇·◇·◇·◇·◇·◇·◇

DATE STARTED: / /

DATE OF
COMPLETION: / /

ADVANCED
INTERMEDIATE
BEGINNER

HOW MUCH I LOVED
THIS PROJECT ♡

◇ ◇ ◇ ◇ ◇

stick picture here

NAME OF
DESIGN:

CANVAS SIZE: _____
PICTURE SIZE: _____
SQUARE DRILL ☐   ROUND DRILL ○

I PURCHASED THIS KIT FROM:
(OR IT WAS GIFTED BY)
_____

PRICE: [_____]

ADVANCED
INTERMEDIATE
BEGINNER

DATE STARTED: / / /
DATE OF
COMPLETION: / / /

HOW MUCH I LOVED
THIS PROJECT ♡
◇ ◇ ◇ ◇ ◇

AFTER THE COMPLETION OF THIS PIECE I:

KEPT IT FOR MYSELF ◇   SOLD IT ◇

GIFTED IT TO A LOVED ONE ◇   OTHER ◇

I GIFTED IT TO: _____
OR I SOLD IT FOR [_____] ON/AT
_____   ON THE / / /

NOTES & IDEAS FOR THE NEXT PROJECT:
_____
_____
_____
_____
_____

stick picture here

◇◦◇◦◇◦◇◦◇◦◇◦◇◦◇◦◇◦◇◦◇◦◇◦◇◦◇◦◇◦◇◦◇

NAME OF
DESIGN:

CANVAS SIZE: _____

PICTURE SIZE: _____

SQUARE DRILL ☐   ROUND DRILL ○

DATE STARTED: / / /

DATE OF
COMPLETION: / / /

I PURCHASED THIS KIT FROM:
(OR IT WAS GIFTED BY)

ADVANCED

INTERMEDIATE

BEGINNER

HOW MUCH I LOVED
THIS PROJECT ♡

◇ ◇ ◇ ◇ ◇

_____

PRICE: [   ]

AFTER THE COMPLETION OF THIS PIECE I:

KEPT IT FOR MYSELF ◇   SOLD IT ◇

GIFTED IT TO A LOVED ONE ◇   OTHER ◇

I GIFTED IT TO: _____

OR I SOLD IT FOR [   ] ON/AT _____

_____ ON THE / / /

NOTES & IDEAS FOR THE NEXT PROJECT:

_____

_____

_____

_____

◇•◇•◇•◇•◇•◇•◇•◇•◇•◇•◇•◇•◇•◇•◇•◇•◇

stick picture here

NAME OF
DESIGN:

CANVAS SIZE: _____

PICTURE SIZE: _____

SQUARE DRILL ☐   ROUND DRILL ○

I PURCHASED THIS KIT FROM:
(OR IT WAS GIFTED BY)

_____

PRICE: [   ]

AFTER THE COMPLETION OF THIS PIECE I:

KEPT IT FOR MYSELF ◇   SOLD IT ◇

GIFTED IT TO A LOVED ONE ◇   OTHER ◇

I GIFTED IT TO: _____
OR I SOLD IT FOR [   ] ON/AT _____
_____ ON THE / / /

NOTES & IDEAS FOR THE NEXT PROJECT:

_____
_____
_____
_____

DATE STARTED: / / /

DATE OF
COMPLETION: / / /

ADVANCED
INTERMEDIATE
BEGINNER

HOW MUCH I LOVED
THIS PROJECT ♡

◇ ◇ ◇ ◇ ◇

stick picture here

◇◇◇◇◇◇◇◇◇◇◇◇◇◇◇◇◇◇◇◇◇

NAME OF
DESIGN:

CANVAS SIZE: _____

PICTURE SIZE: _____

SQUARE DRILL ☐   ROUND DRILL ○

I PURCHASED THIS KIT FROM:
(OR IT WAS GIFTED BY)

_____

PRICE: ☐

AFTER THE COMPLETION OF THIS PIECE I:

KEPT IT FOR MYSELF ◇   SOLD IT ◇

GIFTED IT TO A LOVED ONE ◇   OTHER ◇

I GIFTED IT TO: _____

OR I SOLD IT FOR ☐ ON/AT _____

_____ ON THE / /

NOTES & IDEAS FOR THE NEXT PROJECT:

_____

_____

_____

_____

DATE STARTED: / /

DATE OF
COMPLETION: / /

ADVANCED
INTERMEDIATE
BEGINNER

HOW MUCH I LOVED
THIS PROJECT ♡

◇ ◇ ◇ ◇ ◇

stick picture here

◇·◇·◇·◇·◇·◇·◇·◇·◇·◇·◇·◇·◇·◇·◇·◇·◇·◇·◇

NAME OF
DESIGN:

CANVAS SIZE: _____

PICTURE SIZE: _____

SQUARE DRILL ☐   ROUND DRILL ○

I PURCHASED THIS KIT FROM:
(OR IT WAS GIFTED BY)

_____

PRICE: ☐

ADVANCED

INTERMEDIATE

BEGINNER

DATE STARTED: / / /

DATE OF
COMPLETION: / / /

HOW MUCH I LOVED
THIS PROJECT ♡

◇ ◇ ◇ ◇ ◇

AFTER THE COMPLETION OF THIS PIECE I:

KEPT IT FOR MYSELF ◇   SOLD IT ◇

GIFTED IT TO A LOVED ONE ◇   OTHER ◇

I GIFTED IT TO: _____

OR I SOLD IT FOR ☐ ON/AT _____

_____ ON THE / / /

NOTES & IDEAS FOR THE NEXT PROJECT:

_____

_____

_____

_____

_____

stick picture here

◇◇◇◇◇◇◇◇◇◇◇◇◇◇◇◇◇◇◇◇◇◇◇

NAME OF
DESIGN:

CANVAS SIZE: _____

PICTURE SIZE: _____

SQUARE DRILL ☐   ROUND DRILL ○

I PURCHASED THIS KIT FROM:
(OR IT WAS GIFTED BY)

_____

PRICE: ☐

AFTER THE COMPLETION OF THIS PIECE I:

KEPT IT FOR MYSELF ◇   SOLD IT ◇

GIFTED IT TO A LOVED ONE ◇   OTHER ◇

I GIFTED IT TO:_____
OR I SOLD IT FOR ☐ ON/AT_____

_____ ON THE / / /

NOTES & IDEAS FOR THE NEXT PROJECT:

_____
_____
_____
_____
_____

◇·◇·◇·◇·◇·◇·◇·◇·◇·◇·◇·◇·◇·◇·◇·◇·◇·◇·◇

DATE STARTED: / / /
DATE OF
COMPLETION: / / /

ADVANCED
INTERMEDIATE
BEGINNER

HOW MUCH I LOVED
THIS PROJECT ♡

◇ ◇ ◇ ◇ ◇

stick picture here

NAME OF
DESIGN:

CANVAS SIZE: _____

PICTURE SIZE: _____

SQUARE DRILL ☐   ROUND DRILL ○

DATE STARTED: / / /

DATE OF
COMPLETION: / / /

I PURCHASED THIS KIT FROM:
(OR IT WAS GIFTED BY)

ADVANCED

INTERMEDIATE

BEGINNER

HOW MUCH I LOVED
THIS PROJECT ♡

◇ ◇ ◇ ◇ ◇

_____

PRICE: [   ]

AFTER THE COMPLETION OF THIS PIECE I:

KEPT IT FOR MYSELF ◇   SOLD IT ◇

GIFTED IT TO A LOVED ONE ◇   OTHER ◇

I GIFTED IT TO: _____

OR I SOLD IT FOR [   ] ON/AT _____

_____   ON THE / / /

NOTES & IDEAS FOR THE NEXT PROJECT:

_____

_____

_____

_____

_____

stick picture here

◇•◇•◇•◇•◇•◇•◇•◇•◇•◇•◇•◇•◇•◇•◇•◇•◇

NAME OF
DESIGN:

CANVAS SIZE: _____

PICTURE SIZE: _____

SQUARE DRILL ☐   ROUND DRILL ○

I PURCHASED THIS KIT FROM:
(OR IT WAS GIFTED BY)

_____

PRICE: [_____]

AFTER THE COMPLETION OF THIS PIECE I:

KEPT IT FOR MYSELF ◇   SOLD IT ◇

GIFTED IT TO A LOVED ONE ◇   OTHER ◇

I GIFTED IT TO: _____

OR I SOLD IT FOR [_____] ON/AT _____

_____ ON THE / / /

NOTES & IDEAS FOR THE NEXT PROJECT:

_____

_____

_____

_____

_____

◇·◇·◇·◇·◇·◇·◇·◇·◇·◇·◇·◇·◇·◇·◇·◇·◇·◇

DATE STARTED: / / /

DATE OF
COMPLETION: / / /

ADVANCED
INTERMEDIATE
BEGINNER

HOW MUCH I LOVED
THIS PROJECT ♡

◇ ◇ ◇ ◇ ◇

stick picture here

NAME OF
DESIGN:

CANVAS SIZE: _____

PICTURE SIZE: _____

SQUARE DRILL ☐   ROUND DRILL ○

I PURCHASED THIS KIT FROM:
(OR IT WAS GIFTED BY)

_____

PRICE: [   ]

DATE STARTED: / /

DATE OF
COMPLETION: / /

ADVANCED
INTERMEDIATE
BEGINNER

HOW MUCH I LOVED
THIS PROJECT ♡

◇ ◇ ◇ ◇ ◇

AFTER THE COMPLETION OF THIS PIECE I:

KEPT IT FOR MYSELF ◇   SOLD IT ◇

GIFTED IT TO A LOVED ONE ◇   OTHER ◇

I GIFTED IT TO: _____
OR I SOLD IT FOR [   ] ON/AT _____
_____ ON THE / /

NOTES & IDEAS FOR THE NEXT PROJECT:

_____
_____
_____
_____
_____

stick picture here

◇◇◇◇◇◇◇◇◇◇◇◇◇◇◇◇◇◇◇◇◇◇

NAME OF
DESIGN:

CANVAS SIZE: _____

PICTURE SIZE: _____

SQUARE DRILL ☐   ROUND DRILL ○

DATE STARTED: / / /

DATE OF
COMPLETION: / / /

I PURCHASED THIS KIT FROM:
(OR IT WAS GIFTED BY)

ADVANCED

INTERMEDIATE

BEGINNER

HOW MUCH I LOVED
THIS PROJECT ♡

◇ ◇ ◇ ◇ ◇

_____

PRICE: [   ]

AFTER THE COMPLETION OF THIS PIECE I:

KEPT IT FOR MYSELF ◇   SOLD IT ◇

GIFTED IT TO A LOVED ONE ◇   OTHER ◇

I GIFTED IT TO:_____

OR I SOLD IT FOR [   ] ON/AT_____

_____ ON THE / / /

NOTES & IDEAS FOR THE NEXT PROJECT:

_____

_____

_____

_____

stick picture here

◇•◇•◇•◇•◇•◇•◇•◇•◇•◇•◇•◇•◇•◇◇•◇

NAME OF
DESIGN:

CANVAS SIZE: _____

PICTURE SIZE: _____

SQUARE DRILL ☐   ROUND DRILL ○

DATE STARTED: / / /

DATE OF
COMPLETION: / / /

I PURCHASED THIS KIT FROM:
(OR IT WAS GIFTED BY)

ADVANCED
_____
INTERMEDIATE
_____
BEGINNER

HOW MUCH I LOVED
THIS PROJECT ♡

◇ ◇ ◇ ◇ ◇

_____

PRICE: [   ]

AFTER THE COMPLETION OF THIS PIECE I:

KEPT IT FOR MYSELF ◇   SOLD IT ◇

GIFTED IT TO A LOVED ONE ◇   OTHER ◇

I GIFTED IT TO: _____

OR I SOLD IT FOR [   ] ON/AT _____

_____ ON THE / / /

NOTES & IDEAS FOR THE NEXT PROJECT:

_____

_____

_____

_____

stick picture here

◇·◇·◇·◇·◇·◇·◇·◇·◇·◇·◇·◇·◇·◇·◇·◇·◇·◇·◇

NAME OF
DESIGN:

CANVAS SIZE: _____

PICTURE SIZE: _____

SQUARE DRILL ☐   ROUND DRILL ○

I PURCHASED THIS KIT FROM:
(OR IT WAS GIFTED BY)

_____

PRICE: [   ]

AFTER THE COMPLETION OF THIS PIECE I:

KEPT IT FOR MYSELF ◇   SOLD IT ◇

GIFTED IT TO A LOVED ONE ◇   OTHER ◇

I GIFTED IT TO: _____

OR I SOLD IT FOR [   ] ON/AT _____

_____ ON THE / / /

NOTES & IDEAS FOR THE NEXT PROJECT:

_____
_____
_____
_____
_____

DATE STARTED: / / /

DATE OF
COMPLETION: / / /

ADVANCED
INTERMEDIATE
BEGINNER

HOW MUCH I LOVED
THIS PROJECT ♡

◇ ◇ ◇ ◇ ◇

stick picture here

◇·◇·◇·◇·◇·◇·◇·◇·◇·◇·◇·◇·◇·◇·◇·◇◇◇

NAME OF
DESIGN:

CANVAS SIZE: _____

PICTURE SIZE: _____

SQUARE DRILL ☐   ROUND DRILL ○

DATE STARTED: / / /

DATE OF
COMPLETION: / / /

ADVANCED

INTERMEDIATE

BEGINNER

I PURCHASED THIS KIT FROM:
(OR IT WAS GIFTED BY)

_____

PRICE: [   ]

HOW MUCH I LOVED
THIS PROJECT ♡

◇ ◇ ◇ ◇ ◇

AFTER THE COMPLETION OF THIS PIECE I:

KEPT IT FOR MYSELF ◇   SOLD IT ◇

GIFTED IT TO A LOVED ONE ◇   OTHER ◇

I GIFTED IT TO:_____

OR I SOLD IT FOR [   ] ON/AT _____

_____ ON THE / / /

NOTES & IDEAS FOR THE NEXT PROJECT:

_____
_____
_____
_____

stick picture here

◇·◇·◇·◇·◇·◇·◇·◇·◇·◇·◇·◇·◇·◇·◇·◇·◇·◇·◇

NAME OF
DESIGN:

CANVAS SIZE: _____

PICTURE SIZE: _____

SQUARE DRILL ☐   ROUND DRILL ○

DATE STARTED: / / /

DATE OF
COMPLETION: / / /

I PURCHASED THIS KIT FROM:
(OR IT WAS GIFTED BY)

ADVANCED

INTERMEDIATE

BEGINNER

HOW MUCH I LOVED
THIS PROJECT ♡

◇ ◇ ◇ ◇ ◇

_____

PRICE: [   ]

AFTER THE COMPLETION OF THIS PIECE I:

KEPT IT FOR MYSELF ◇   SOLD IT ◇

GIFTED IT TO A LOVED ONE ◇   OTHER ◇

I GIFTED IT TO:_____

OR I SOLD IT FOR [   ] ON/AT_____

_____ ON THE / / /

NOTES & IDEAS FOR THE NEXT PROJECT:

_____

_____

_____

_____

◇·◇·◇·◇·◇·◇·◇·◇·◇·◇·◇·◇·◇·◇·◇◇·◇

stick picture here

NAME OF
DESIGN:

CANVAS SIZE: _____

PICTURE SIZE: _____

SQUARE DRILL ☐   ROUND DRILL ○

I PURCHASED THIS KIT FROM:
(OR IT WAS GIFTED BY)

ADVANCED

INTERMEDIATE

BEGINNER

_____
PRICE: [_____]

AFTER THE COMPLETION OF THIS PIECE I:

KEPT IT FOR MYSELF ◇   SOLD IT ◇

GIFTED IT TO A LOVED ONE ◇   OTHER ◇

I GIFTED IT TO: _____

OR I SOLD IT FOR [_____] ON/AT _____

_____ ON THE / / /

NOTES & IDEAS FOR THE NEXT PROJECT:

_____

_____

_____

_____

DATE STARTED: / / /

DATE OF
COMPLETION: / / /

HOW MUCH I LOVED
THIS PROJECT ♡

◇ ◇ ◇ ◇ ◇

stick picture here

◇·◇

NAME OF
DESIGN:

CANVAS SIZE: _____

PICTURE SIZE: _____

SQUARE DRILL ☐   ROUND DRILL ◯

I PURCHASED THIS KIT FROM:
(OR IT WAS GIFTED BY)

_____

PRICE: [   ]

DATE STARTED: / / /

DATE OF
COMPLETION: / / /

ADVANCED
INTERMEDIATE
BEGINNER

HOW MUCH I LOVED
THIS PROJECT ♡
◇ ◇ ◇ ◇ ◇

AFTER THE COMPLETION OF THIS PIECE I:

KEPT IT FOR MYSELF ◇   SOLD IT ◇

GIFTED IT TO A LOVED ONE ◇   OTHER ◇

I GIFTED IT TO: _____

OR I SOLD IT FOR [   ] ON/AT _____

_____ ON THE / / /

NOTES & IDEAS FOR THE NEXT PROJECT:

_____
_____
_____
_____
_____

◇·◇·◇·◇ ◇ ◇ ◇ ◇·◇·◇·◇·◇ ◇ ◇ ◇◇◇·◇

stick picture here

NAME OF
DESIGN:

CANVAS SIZE: _____

PICTURE SIZE: _____

SQUARE DRILL ☐   ROUND DRILL ○

I PURCHASED THIS KIT FROM:
(OR IT WAS GIFTED BY)

_____

PRICE: [_____]

ADVANCED

INTERMEDIATE

BEGINNER

DATE STARTED: / / /

DATE OF
COMPLETION: / / /

HOW MUCH I LOVED
THIS PROJECT ♡

◇ ◇ ◇ ◇ ◇

AFTER THE COMPLETION OF THIS PIECE I:

KEPT IT FOR MYSELF ◇   SOLD IT ◇

GIFTED IT TO A LOVED ONE ◇   OTHER ◇

I GIFTED IT TO: _____

OR I SOLD IT FOR [_____] ON/AT _____

_____ ON THE / / /

NOTES & IDEAS FOR THE NEXT PROJECT:

_____
_____
_____
_____
_____
_____

stick picture here

◇·◇·◇·◇·◇·◇·◇·◇·◇·◇·◇·◇·◇·◇·◇·◇·◇·◇

NAME OF
DESIGN:

CANVAS SIZE: _____

PICTURE SIZE: _____

SQUARE DRILL ☐   ROUND DRILL ○

I PURCHASED THIS KIT FROM:
(OR IT WAS GIFTED BY)

_____

PRICE: [   ]

AFTER THE COMPLETION OF THIS PIECE I:

KEPT IT FOR MYSELF ◇   SOLD IT ◇

GIFTED IT TO A LOVED ONE ◇   OTHER ◇

I GIFTED IT TO: _____

OR I SOLD IT FOR [   ] ON/AT _____

_____   ON THE / /

NOTES & IDEAS FOR THE NEXT PROJECT:

_____
_____
_____
_____
_____

◇·◇·◇·◇·◇·◇·◇·◇·◇·◇·◇·◇·◇·◇·◇·◇·◇·◇·◇·◇

DATE STARTED: / /

DATE OF
COMPLETION: / /

ADVANCED

INTERMEDIATE

BEGINNER

HOW MUCH I LOVED
THIS PROJECT ♡

◇ ◇ ◇ ◇ ◇

stick picture here

NAME OF DESIGN:

CANVAS SIZE: _____

PICTURE SIZE: _____

SQUARE DRILL ☐   ROUND DRILL ○

I PURCHASED THIS KIT FROM:
(OR IT WAS GIFTED BY)

_____

PRICE: [＿＿＿＿]

DATE STARTED: / / /

DATE OF
COMPLETION: / / /

ADVANCED
INTERMEDIATE
BEGINNER

HOW MUCH I LOVED
THIS PROJECT ♡
◇ ◇ ◇ ◇ ◇

AFTER THE COMPLETION OF THIS PIECE I:

KEPT IT FOR MYSELF ◇   SOLD IT ◇

GIFTED IT TO A LOVED ONE ◇   OTHER ◇

I GIFTED IT TO: _____
OR I SOLD IT FOR [＿＿＿] ON/AT _____

_____ ON THE / / /

NOTES & IDEAS FOR THE NEXT PROJECT:

_____
_____
_____
_____
_____

stick picture here

◇·◇·◇·◇·◇·◇·◇·◇·◇·◇·◇·◇·◇·◇·◇·◇

NAME OF
DESIGN:

CANVAS SIZE: _____

PICTURE SIZE: _____

SQUARE DRILL ☐   ROUND DRILL ○

I PURCHASED THIS KIT FROM:
(OR IT WAS GIFTED BY)

_____

PRICE: [＿＿＿＿]

AFTER THE COMPLETION OF THIS PIECE I:

KEPT IT FOR MYSELF ◇   SOLD IT ◇

GIFTED IT TO A LOVED ONE ◇   OTHER ◇

I GIFTED IT TO:_____

OR I SOLD IT FOR [＿＿＿] ON/AT_____

_____ ON THE / /

NOTES & IDEAS FOR THE NEXT PROJECT:

_____
_____
_____
_____
_____

◇·◇·◇·◇·◇·◇·◇·◇·◇·◇·◇·◇·◇·◇·◇·◇·◇·◇·◇

ADVANCED

INTERMEDIATE

BEGINNER

DATE STARTED: / /

DATE OF
COMPLETION: / /

HOW MUCH I LOVED
THIS PROJECT ♡

◇ ◇ ◇ ◇ ◇

stick picture here

NAME OF
DESIGN:

CANVAS SIZE: _____

PICTURE SIZE: _____

SQUARE DRILL ☐   ROUND DRILL ○

I PURCHASED THIS KIT FROM:
(OR IT WAS GIFTED BY)

ADVANCED

INTERMEDIATE

BEGINNER

PRICE: [_____]

AFTER THE COMPLETION OF THIS PIECE I:

KEPT IT FOR MYSELF ◇   SOLD IT ◇

GIFTED IT TO A LOVED ONE ◇   OTHER ◇

I GIFTED IT TO: _____

OR I SOLD IT FOR [_____] ON/AT _____

_____ ON THE / / /

NOTES & IDEAS FOR THE NEXT PROJECT:

_____

_____

_____

_____

DATE STARTED: / / /

DATE OF
COMPLETION: / / /

HOW MUCH I LOVED
THIS PROJECT ♡

◇ ◇ ◇ ◇ ◇

stick picture here

◇•◇•◇•◇•◇•◇•◇•◇•◇•◇•◇•◇•◇•◇•◇•◇•◇•◇•

NAME OF DESIGN:

CANVAS SIZE: _____

PICTURE SIZE: _____

SQUARE DRILL ☐   ROUND DRILL ○

I PURCHASED THIS KIT FROM:
(OR IT WAS GIFTED BY)

_____

PRICE: [_____]

DATE STARTED: / / /

DATE OF
COMPLETION: / / /

ADVANCED
INTERMEDIATE
BEGINNER

HOW MUCH I LOVED
THIS PROJECT ♡

◇ ◇ ◇ ◇ ◇

AFTER THE COMPLETION OF THIS PIECE I:

KEPT IT FOR MYSELF ◇   SOLD IT ◇

GIFTED IT TO A LOVED ONE ◇   OTHER ◇

I GIFTED IT TO: _____

OR I SOLD IT FOR [_____] ON/AT _____

_____ ON THE / / /

NOTES & IDEAS FOR THE NEXT PROJECT:

_____
_____
_____
_____

◇•◇•◇•◇•◇•◇•◇•◇•◇•◇•◇•◇•◇•◇•◇•◇

stick picture here

NAME OF
DESIGN:

CANVAS SIZE: _____

PICTURE SIZE: _____

SQUARE DRILL ☐   ROUND DRILL ○

I PURCHASED THIS KIT FROM:
(OR IT WAS GIFTED BY)

_____

PRICE: [   ]

AFTER THE COMPLETION OF THIS PIECE I:

KEPT IT FOR MYSELF ◇   SOLD IT ◇

GIFTED IT TO A LOVED ONE ◇   OTHER ◇

I GIFTED IT TO: _____
OR I SOLD IT FOR [   ] ON/AT _____
_____ ON THE / / /

NOTES & IDEAS FOR THE NEXT PROJECT:

_____
_____
_____
_____

DATE STARTED: / / /
DATE OF
COMPLETION: / / /

ADVANCED
INTERMEDIATE
BEGINNER

HOW MUCH I LOVED
THIS PROJECT ♡
◇ ◇ ◇ ◇ ◇

stick picture here

◇•◇•◇•◇•◇•◇•◇•◇•◇•◇•◇•◇•◇•◇◇•◇

NAME OF DESIGN:

CANVAS SIZE: _____

PICTURE SIZE: _____

SQUARE DRILL ☐   ROUND DRILL ○

I PURCHASED THIS KIT FROM:
(OR IT WAS GIFTED BY)

_____

PRICE: [   ]

DATE STARTED: / / /

DATE OF COMPLETION: / / /

ADVANCED
INTERMEDIATE
BEGINNER

HOW MUCH I LOVED THIS PROJECT ♡

◇ ◇ ◇ ◇ ◇

AFTER THE COMPLETION OF THIS PIECE I:

KEPT IT FOR MYSELF ◇   SOLD IT ◇

GIFTED IT TO A LOVED ONE ◇   OTHER ◇

I GIFTED IT TO: _____

OR I SOLD IT FOR [   ] ON/AT _____

_____ ON THE / / /

NOTES & IDEAS FOR THE NEXT PROJECT:

_____
_____
_____
_____
_____

stick picture here

◇·◇·◇·◇·◇·◇·◇·◇·◇·◇·◇·◇·◇·◇·◇·◇·◇·◇

NAME OF DESIGN:

CANVAS SIZE: _____

PICTURE SIZE: _____

SQUARE DRILL ☐   ROUND DRILL ○

DATE STARTED: / / /

DATE OF COMPLETION: / / /

I PURCHASED THIS KIT FROM:
(OR IT WAS GIFTED BY)

ADVANCED
INTERMEDIATE
BEGINNER

HOW MUCH I LOVED THIS PROJECT ♡
◇ ◇ ◇ ◇ ◇

PRICE: [ ]

AFTER THE COMPLETION OF THIS PIECE I:

KEPT IT FOR MYSELF ◇   SOLD IT ◇

GIFTED IT TO A LOVED ONE ◇   OTHER ◇

I GIFTED IT TO: _____

OR I SOLD IT FOR [ ] ON/AT _____

_____ ON THE / / /

NOTES & IDEAS FOR THE NEXT PROJECT:

_____

_____

_____

_____

◇·◇·◇·◇·◇·◇·◇·◇·◇·◇·◇·◇·◇·◇·◇·◇·◇·◇

stick picture here

NAME OF
DESIGN:

CANVAS SIZE: _____

PICTURE SIZE: _____

SQUARE DRILL ☐   ROUND DRILL ○

DATE STARTED: / / /

DATE OF
COMPLETION: / / /

I PURCHASED THIS KIT FROM:
(OR IT WAS GIFTED BY)

ADVANCED

INTERMEDIATE

BEGINNER

HOW MUCH I LOVED
THIS PROJECT ♥

◇ ◇ ◇ ◇ ◇

_____

PRICE: [   ]

AFTER THE COMPLETION OF THIS PIECE I:

KEPT IT FOR MYSELF ◇   SOLD IT ◇

GIFTED IT TO A LOVED ONE ◇   OTHER ◇

I GIFTED IT TO:_____

OR I SOLD IT FOR [   ] ON/AT_____

_____ ON THE / / /

NOTES & IDEAS FOR THE NEXT PROJECT:

_____

_____

_____

_____

◇·◇·◇·◇·◇·◇·◇·◇·◇·◇·◇·◇·◇·◇·◇·◇

stick picture here

NAME OF
DESIGN:

CANVAS SIZE: _____

PICTURE SIZE: _____

SQUARE DRILL ☐   ROUND DRILL ○

I PURCHASED THIS KIT FROM:
(OR IT WAS GIFTED BY)

_____

PRICE: [   ]

DATE STARTED: / / /

DATE OF
COMPLETION: / / /

ADVANCED

INTERMEDIATE

BEGINNER

HOW MUCH I LOVED
THIS PROJECT ♡

◇ ◇ ◇ ◇ ◇

AFTER THE COMPLETION OF THIS PIECE I:

KEPT IT FOR MYSELF ◇   SOLD IT ◇

GIFTED IT TO A LOVED ONE ◇   OTHER ◇

I GIFTED IT TO: _____

OR I SOLD IT FOR [   ] ON/AT _____

_____ ON THE / / /

NOTES & IDEAS FOR THE NEXT PROJECT:

_____

_____

_____

_____

stick picture here

◇·◇·◇·◇·◇·◇·◇·◇·◇·◇·◇·◇·◇·◇·◇·◇·◇·◇·◇·◇

NAME OF DESIGN:

CANVAS SIZE: _____

PICTURE SIZE: _____

SQUARE DRILL ☐   ROUND DRILL ○

I PURCHASED THIS KIT FROM:
(OR IT WAS GIFTED BY)

_____

PRICE: ☐

AFTER THE COMPLETION OF THIS PIECE I:

KEPT IT FOR MYSELF ◇   SOLD IT ◇

GIFTED IT TO A LOVED ONE ◇   OTHER ◇

I GIFTED IT TO: _____

OR I SOLD IT FOR ☐ ON/AT _____

_____ ON THE / / /

NOTES & IDEAS FOR THE NEXT PROJECT:

_____
_____
_____
_____

◇·◇·◇·◇·◇·◇·◇·◇·◇·◇·◇·◇·◇·◇·◇

DATE STARTED: / / /

DATE OF COMPLETION: / / /

ADVANCED
INTERMEDIATE
BEGINNER

HOW MUCH I LOVED THIS PROJECT ♡
◇ ◇ ◇ ◇ ◇

stick picture here

NAME OF
DESIGN:

CANVAS SIZE: _____

PICTURE SIZE: _____

SQUARE DRILL ☐   ROUND DRILL ○

DATE STARTED: / / /

DATE OF
COMPLETION: / / /

I PURCHASED THIS KIT FROM:
(OR IT WAS GIFTED BY)

_____

PRICE: [_____]

ADVANCED

INTERMEDIATE

BEGINNER

HOW MUCH I LOVED
THIS PROJECT ♡

◇ ◇ ◇ ◇ ◇

AFTER THE COMPLETION OF THIS PIECE I:

KEPT IT FOR MYSELF ◇   SOLD IT ◇

GIFTED IT TO A LOVED ONE ◇   OTHER ◇

I GIFTED IT TO: _____

OR I SOLD IT FOR [_____] ON/AT _____

_____ ON THE / / /

NOTES & IDEAS FOR THE NEXT PROJECT:

_____

_____

_____

_____

stick picture here

◇•◇•◇•◇•◇•◇•◇•◇•◇•◇•◇•◇•◇•◇•◇•◇•◇•◇•

NAME OF
DESIGN:

CANVAS SIZE: _____

PICTURE SIZE: _____

SQUARE DRILL ☐   ROUND DRILL ○

I PURCHASED THIS KIT FROM:
(OR IT WAS GIFTED BY)

_____

PRICE: [   ]

DATE STARTED: / / /

DATE OF
COMPLETION: / / /

ADVANCED

INTERMEDIATE

BEGINNER

HOW MUCH I LOVED
THIS PROJECT ♥

◇ ◇ ◇ ◇ ◇

AFTER THE COMPLETION OF THIS PIECE I:

KEPT IT FOR MYSELF ◇   SOLD IT ◇

GIFTED IT TO A LOVED ONE ◇   OTHER ◇

I GIFTED IT TO: _____

OR I SOLD IT FOR [   ] ON/AT _____

_____ ON THE / / /

NOTES & IDEAS FOR THE NEXT PROJECT:

_____
_____
_____
_____
_____

◇·◇·◇·◇·◇·◇·◇·◇·◇·◇·◇·◇·◇·◇·◇·◇·◇·◇·◇

stick picture here

NAME OF DESIGN:

CANVAS SIZE: _____

PICTURE SIZE: _____

SQUARE DRILL ☐   ROUND DRILL ○

DATE STARTED: / / /

DATE OF COMPLETION: / / /

I PURCHASED THIS KIT FROM:
(OR IT WAS GIFTED BY)

ADVANCED
INTERMEDIATE
BEGINNER

HOW MUCH I LOVED THIS PROJECT ♡
◇ ◇ ◇ ◇ ◇

_____

PRICE: [   ]

AFTER THE COMPLETION OF THIS PIECE I:

KEPT IT FOR MYSELF ◇   SOLD IT ◇

GIFTED IT TO A LOVED ONE ◇   OTHER ◇

I GIFTED IT TO: _____
OR I SOLD IT FOR [   ] ON/AT _____
_____ ON THE / / /

NOTES & IDEAS FOR THE NEXT PROJECT:

_____
_____
_____
_____
_____

stick picture here

◇◇◇◇◇ ◇◇◇◇◇ ◇◇◇◇◇ ◇◇◇◇◇

NAME OF
DESIGN:

CANVAS SIZE: _____

PICTURE SIZE: _____

SQUARE DRILL ☐   ROUND DRILL ○

I PURCHASED THIS KIT FROM:
(OR IT WAS GIFTED BY)

_____

PRICE: [   ]

AFTER THE COMPLETION OF THIS PIECE I:

KEPT IT FOR MYSELF ◇   SOLD IT ◇

GIFTED IT TO A LOVED ONE ◇   OTHER ◇

I GIFTED IT TO: _____

OR I SOLD IT FOR [   ] ON/AT _____

_____ ON THE / / /

NOTES & IDEAS FOR THE NEXT PROJECT:

_____
_____
_____
_____

DATE STARTED: / / /

DATE OF
COMPLETION: / / /

ADVANCED
INTERMEDIATE
BEGINNER

HOW MUCH I LOVED
THIS PROJECT ♡

◇ ◇ ◇ ◇ ◇

stick picture here

◇·◇·◇·◇·◇·◇·◇·◇·◇·◇·◇·◇·◇·◇·◇·◇·◇·◇·◇

NAME OF
DESIGN:

CANVAS SIZE: _____

PICTURE SIZE: _____

SQUARE DRILL ☐   ROUND DRILL ○

DATE STARTED: / / /

DATE OF
COMPLETION: / / /

I PURCHASED THIS KIT FROM:
(OR IT WAS GIFTED BY)

ADVANCED

INTERMEDIATE

BEGINNER

HOW MUCH I LOVED
THIS PROJECT ♡
◇ ◇ ◇ ◇ ◇

_____

PRICE: [_____]

AFTER THE COMPLETION OF THIS PIECE I:

KEPT IT FOR MYSELF ◇   SOLD IT ◇

GIFTED IT TO A LOVED ONE ◇   OTHER ◇

I GIFTED IT TO: _____
OR I SOLD IT FOR [_____] ON/AT _____

_____ ON THE / / /

NOTES & IDEAS FOR THE NEXT PROJECT:

_____

_____

_____

_____

stick picture here

◇◦◇◦◇◦◇◦◇◦◇◦◇◦◇◦◇◦◇◦◇◦◇◦◇◦◇

NAME OF DESIGN:

CANVAS SIZE: _____

PICTURE SIZE: _____

SQUARE DRILL ☐   ROUND DRILL ○

I PURCHASED THIS KIT FROM:
(OR IT WAS GIFTED BY)

_____

PRICE: [＿＿＿＿]

DATE STARTED: / / /

DATE OF
COMPLETION: / / /

ADVANCED

INTERMEDIATE

BEGINNER

HOW MUCH I LOVED
THIS PROJECT ♡

◇ ◇ ◇ ◇ ◇

AFTER THE COMPLETION OF THIS PIECE I:

KEPT IT FOR MYSELF ◇   SOLD IT ◇

GIFTED IT TO A LOVED ONE ◇   OTHER ◇

I GIFTED IT TO:_____

OR I SOLD IT FOR [＿＿＿] ON/AT_____

_____ ON THE / / /

NOTES & IDEAS FOR THE NEXT PROJECT:

_____
_____
_____
_____
_____

◇·◇·◇·◇·◇·◇·◇·◇·◇·◇·◇·◇·◇·◇·◇·◇·◇

stick picture here

NAME OF
DESIGN:

CANVAS SIZE: _____

PICTURE SIZE: _____

SQUARE DRILL ☐   ROUND DRILL ○

DATE STARTED: / / /

DATE OF
COMPLETION: / / /

I PURCHASED THIS KIT FROM:
(OR IT WAS GIFTED BY)

ADVANCED

INTERMEDIATE

BEGINNER

HOW MUCH I LOVED
THIS PROJECT ♡

◇ ◇ ◇ ◇ ◇

_____

PRICE: [   ]

AFTER THE COMPLETION OF THIS PIECE I:

KEPT IT FOR MYSELF ◇ SOLD IT ◇

GIFTED IT TO A LOVED ONE ◇ OTHER ◇

I GIFTED IT TO:_____

OR I SOLD IT FOR [   ] ON/AT _____

_____ ON THE / / /

NOTES & IDEAS FOR THE NEXT PROJECT:

_____

_____

_____

_____

_____

stick picture here

◇•◇•◇•◇•◇•◇•◇•◇•◇•◇•◇•◇•◇•◇•◇•◇

NAME OF
DESIGN:

CANVAS SIZE: _____

PICTURE SIZE: _____

SQUARE DRILL ☐   ROUND DRILL ○

I PURCHASED THIS KIT FROM:
(OR IT WAS GIFTED BY)

_____

PRICE: [_____]

ADVANCED

INTERMEDIATE

BEGINNER

DATE STARTED: / / /

DATE OF
COMPLETION: / / /

HOW MUCH I LOVED
THIS PROJECT ♡

◇ ◇ ◇ ◇ ◇

AFTER THE COMPLETION OF THIS PIECE I:

KEPT IT FOR MYSELF ◇   SOLD IT ◇

GIFTED IT TO A LOVED ONE ◇   OTHER ◇

I GIFTED IT TO: _____

OR I SOLD IT FOR [_____] ON/AT _____

_____ ON THE / / /

NOTES & IDEAS FOR THE NEXT PROJECT:

_____
_____
_____
_____
_____

stick picture here

◇·◇

NAME OF DESIGN:

CANVAS SIZE: _____

PICTURE SIZE: _____

SQUARE DRILL ☐   ROUND DRILL ○

DATE STARTED: / / /

DATE OF COMPLETION: / / /

I PURCHASED THIS KIT FROM:
(OR IT WAS GIFTED BY)

ADVANCED

INTERMEDIATE

BEGINNER

HOW MUCH I LOVED THIS PROJECT ♡

◇ ◇ ◇ ◇ ◇

_____

PRICE: [   ]

AFTER THE COMPLETION OF THIS PIECE I:

KEPT IT FOR MYSELF ◇   SOLD IT ◇

GIFTED IT TO A LOVED ONE ◇   OTHER ◇

I GIFTED IT TO: _____

OR I SOLD IT FOR [   ] ON/AT _____

_____ ON THE / / /

NOTES & IDEAS FOR THE NEXT PROJECT:

_____

_____

_____

_____

stick picture here

◇◦◇◦◇◦◇◦◇◦◇◦◇◦◇◦◇◦◇◦◇◦◇◦◇◦◇◦◇

NAME OF
DESIGN:

CANVAS SIZE: _____

PICTURE SIZE: _____

SQUARE DRILL ☐   ROUND DRILL ○

DATE STARTED: / / /

DATE OF
COMPLETION: / / /

ADVANCED
INTERMEDIATE
BEGINNER

I PURCHASED THIS KIT FROM:
(OR IT WAS GIFTED BY)

_____

PRICE: [   ]

HOW MUCH I LOVED
THIS PROJECT ♡

◇ ◇ ◇ ◇ ◇

AFTER THE COMPLETION OF THIS PIECE I:

KEPT IT FOR MYSELF ◇   SOLD IT ◇

GIFTED IT TO A LOVED ONE ◇   OTHER ◇

I GIFTED IT TO:_____

OR I SOLD IT FOR [   ] ON/AT_____

_____ ON THE / / /

NOTES & IDEAS FOR THE NEXT PROJECT:

_____

_____

_____

_____

_____

stick picture here

◇◇◇◇◇◇◇◇◇◇◇◇◇◇◇◇◇◇◇◇

NAME OF
DESIGN:

CANVAS SIZE: _____

PICTURE SIZE: _____

SQUARE DRILL ☐   ROUND DRILL ○

I PURCHASED THIS KIT FROM:
(OR IT WAS GIFTED BY)

_____

PRICE: [   ]

ADVANCED
INTERMEDIATE
BEGINNER

DATE STARTED: / / /

DATE OF
COMPLETION: / / /

HOW MUCH I LOVED
THIS PROJECT ♡
◇ ◇ ◇ ◇ ◇

AFTER THE COMPLETION OF THIS PIECE I:

KEPT IT FOR MYSELF ◇   SOLD IT ◇

GIFTED IT TO A LOVED ONE ◇   OTHER ◇

I GIFTED IT TO: _____

OR I SOLD IT FOR [   ] ON/AT _____

_____ ON THE / / /

NOTES & IDEAS FOR THE NEXT PROJECT:

_____

_____

_____

_____

stick picture here

◇·◇·◇·◇·◇·◇·◇·◇·◇·◇·◇·◇·◇·◇·◇·◇·◇·◇

NAME OF
DESIGN:

CANVAS SIZE: _____

PICTURE SIZE: _____

SQUARE DRILL ☐   ROUND DRILL ◯

I PURCHASED THIS KIT FROM:
(OR IT WAS GIFTED BY)

_____

PRICE: [   ]

DATE STARTED: / / /

DATE OF
COMPLETION: / / /

ADVANCED
INTERMEDIATE
BEGINNER

HOW MUCH I LOVED
THIS PROJECT ♡

◇ ◇ ◇ ◇ ◇

AFTER THE COMPLETION OF THIS PIECE I:

KEPT IT FOR MYSELF ◇   SOLD IT ◇

GIFTED IT TO A LOVED ONE ◇   OTHER ◇

I GIFTED IT TO: _____

OR I SOLD IT FOR [   ] ON/AT _____

_____ ON THE / / /

NOTES & IDEAS FOR THE NEXT PROJECT:

_____
_____
_____
_____

◇·◇·◇·◇·◇·◇·◇·◇·◇·◇·◇·◇·◇·◇·◇·◇·◇·◇

stick picture here

NAME OF
DESIGN:

CANVAS SIZE: _____

PICTURE SIZE: _____

SQUARE DRILL ☐   ROUND DRILL ○

I PURCHASED THIS KIT FROM:
(OR IT WAS GIFTED BY)

_____

PRICE: [   ]

AFTER THE COMPLETION OF THIS PIECE I:

KEPT IT FOR MYSELF ◇   SOLD IT ◇

GIFTED IT TO A LOVED ONE ◇   OTHER ◇

I GIFTED IT TO: _____
OR I SOLD IT FOR [   ] ON/AT
_____ ON THE / / /

NOTES & IDEAS FOR THE NEXT PROJECT:

_____
_____
_____
_____
_____

DATE STARTED: / / /
DATE OF
COMPLETION: / / /

ADVANCED
INTERMEDIATE
BEGINNER

HOW MUCH I LOVED
THIS PROJECT ♡
◇ ◇ ◇ ◇ ◇

stick picture here

◇·◇·◇·◇·◇·◇·◇·◇·◇·◇·◇·◇·◇·◇·◇·◇·◇

NAME OF
DESIGN:

CANVAS SIZE: _____
PICTURE SIZE: _____
SQUARE DRILL ☐   ROUND DRILL ○

I PURCHASED THIS KIT FROM:
(OR IT WAS GIFTED BY)

_____

PRICE: [   ]

DATE STARTED: / / /
DATE OF
COMPLETION: / / /

ADVANCED
INTERMEDIATE
BEGINNER

HOW MUCH I LOVED
THIS PROJECT ♡
◇ ◇ ◇ ◇ ◇

AFTER THE COMPLETION OF THIS PIECE I:

KEPT IT FOR MYSELF ◇   SOLD IT ◇

GIFTED IT TO A LOVED ONE ◇   OTHER ◇

I GIFTED IT TO: _____
OR I SOLD IT FOR [   ] ON/AT _____
_____ ON THE / / /

NOTES & IDEAS FOR THE NEXT PROJECT:

_____
_____
_____
_____
_____

stick picture here

◇·◇·◇·◇·◇·◇·◇·◇·◇·◇·◇·◇·◇·◇·◇·◇·◇·◇·◇

NAME OF DESIGN:

CANVAS SIZE: _____

PICTURE SIZE: _____

SQUARE DRILL ☐   ROUND DRILL ○

I PURCHASED THIS KIT FROM:
(OR IT WAS GIFTED BY)

_____

PRICE: [_____]

ADVANCED
INTERMEDIATE
BEGINNER

DATE STARTED: / / /

DATE OF
COMPLETION: / / /

HOW MUCH I LOVED
THIS PROJECT ♡

◇ ◇ ◇ ◇ ◇

AFTER THE COMPLETION OF THIS PIECE I:

KEPT IT FOR MYSELF ◇   SOLD IT ◇

GIFTED IT TO A LOVED ONE ◇   OTHER ◇

I GIFTED IT TO: _____

OR I SOLD IT FOR [_____] ON/AT _____

_____ ON THE / / /

NOTES & IDEAS FOR THE NEXT PROJECT:

_____

_____

_____

_____

stick picture here

◇·◇·◇·◇·◇·◇·◇·◇·◇·◇·◇·◇·◇·◇·◇·◇·◇·◇

NAME OF
DESIGN:

CANVAS SIZE: _____

PICTURE SIZE: _____

SQUARE DRILL ☐   ROUND DRILL ○

DATE STARTED: / / /

DATE OF
COMPLETION: / / /

I PURCHASED THIS KIT FROM:
(OR IT WAS GIFTED BY)

_____

PRICE: [   ]

ADVANCED
INTERMEDIATE
BEGINNER

HOW MUCH I LOVED
THIS PROJECT ♡

◇ ◇ ◇ ◇ ◇

AFTER THE COMPLETION OF THIS PIECE I:

KEPT IT FOR MYSELF ◇   SOLD IT ◇

GIFTED IT TO A LOVED ONE ◇   OTHER ◇

I GIFTED IT TO: _____

OR I SOLD IT FOR [   ] ON/AT _____

_____ ON THE / / /

NOTES & IDEAS FOR THE NEXT PROJECT:

_____

_____

_____

_____

◇·◇·◇·◇·◇·◇·◇·◇·◇·◇·◇·◇·◇·◇·◇·◇·◇

stick picture here

NAME OF
DESIGN:

CANVAS SIZE: _____

PICTURE SIZE: _____

SQUARE DRILL ☐   ROUND DRILL ◯

I PURCHASED THIS KIT FROM:
(OR IT WAS GIFTED BY)

_____

PRICE: [   ]

DATE STARTED: / / /

DATE OF
COMPLETION: / / /

ADVANCED
INTERMEDIATE
BEGINNER

HOW MUCH I LOVED
THIS PROJECT ♡

◇ ◇ ◇ ◇ ◇

AFTER THE COMPLETION OF THIS PIECE I:

KEPT IT FOR MYSELF ◇   SOLD IT ◇

GIFTED IT TO A LOVED ONE ◇   OTHER ◇

I GIFTED IT TO: _____

OR I SOLD IT FOR [   ] ON/AT _____

_____ ON THE / / /

NOTES & IDEAS FOR THE NEXT PROJECT:

_____

_____

_____

_____

_____

stick picture here

◇·◇

NAME OF
DESIGN:

CANVAS SIZE: _____

PICTURE SIZE: _____

SQUARE DRILL ☐   ROUND DRILL ○

I PURCHASED THIS KIT FROM:
(OR IT WAS GIFTED BY)

_____

PRICE: [   ]

DATE STARTED: / / /

DATE OF
COMPLETION: / / /

ADVANCED

INTERMEDIATE

BEGINNER

HOW MUCH I LOVED
THIS PROJECT ♡

◇ ◇ ◇ ◇ ◇

AFTER THE COMPLETION OF THIS PIECE I:

KEPT IT FOR MYSELF ◇   SOLD IT ◇

GIFTED IT TO A LOVED ONE ◇   OTHER ◇

I GIFTED IT TO:_____

OR I SOLD IT FOR [   ] ON/AT

_____ ON THE / / /

NOTES & IDEAS FOR THE NEXT PROJECT:

_____
_____
_____
_____

◇◦◇◦◇◦◇◦◇◦◇◦◇◦◇◦◇◦◇◦◇◦◇◦◇◦◇◦◇◦◇

stick picture here

NAME OF
DESIGN:

CANVAS SIZE: _____

PICTURE SIZE: _____

SQUARE DRILL ☐   ROUND DRILL ○

I PURCHASED THIS KIT FROM:
(OR IT WAS GIFTED BY)

_____

PRICE: [_____]

AFTER THE COMPLETION OF THIS PIECE I:

KEPT IT FOR MYSELF ◇   SOLD IT ◇

GIFTED IT TO A LOVED ONE ◇   OTHER ◇

I GIFTED IT TO: _____
OR I SOLD IT FOR [_____] ON/AT _____
_____ ON THE / / /

NOTES & IDEAS FOR THE NEXT PROJECT:

_____
_____
_____
_____
_____

DATE STARTED: / / /
DATE OF
COMPLETION: / / /

ADVANCED
INTERMEDIATE
BEGINNER

HOW MUCH I LOVED
THIS PROJECT ♡
◇ ◇ ◇ ◇ ◇

stick picture here

◇◦◇◦◇◦◇◦◇◦◇◦◇◦◇◦◇◦◇◦◇◦◇◦◇◦◇◦◇◦◇

NAME OF
DESIGN:

CANVAS SIZE: _____

PICTURE SIZE: _____

SQUARE DRILL ☐   ROUND DRILL ○

DATE STARTED: / / /

DATE OF
COMPLETION: / / /

I PURCHASED THIS KIT FROM:
(OR IT WAS GIFTED BY)

ADVANCED
INTERMEDIATE
BEGINNER

HOW MUCH I LOVED
THIS PROJECT ♡

◇ ◇ ◇ ◇ ◇

_____

PRICE: [   ]

AFTER THE COMPLETION OF THIS PIECE I:

KEPT IT FOR MYSELF ◇   SOLD IT ◇

GIFTED IT TO A LOVED ONE ◇   OTHER ◇

I GIFTED IT TO: _____

OR I SOLD IT FOR [   ] ON/AT _____

_____ ON THE / / /

NOTES & IDEAS FOR THE NEXT PROJECT:

_____

_____

_____

_____

stick picture here

◇◇◇◇◇◇◇◇◇◇◇◇◇◇◇◇◇◇◇

NAME OF
DESIGN:

CANVAS SIZE: _____

PICTURE SIZE: _____

SQUARE DRILL ☐   ROUND DRILL ○

DATE STARTED: / / /

DATE OF
COMPLETION: / / /

I PURCHASED THIS KIT FROM:
(OR IT WAS GIFTED BY)

ADVANCED

INTERMEDIATE

BEGINNER

HOW MUCH I LOVED
THIS PROJECT ♡

◇ ◇ ◇ ◇ ◇

PRICE: [   ]

AFTER THE COMPLETION OF THIS PIECE I:

KEPT IT FOR MYSELF ◇   SOLD IT ◇

GIFTED IT TO A LOVED ONE ◇   OTHER ◇

I GIFTED IT TO: _____

OR I SOLD IT FOR [   ] ON/AT _____

_____ ON THE / / /

NOTES & IDEAS FOR THE NEXT PROJECT:

_____

_____

_____

_____

stick picture here

◇◇◇◇◇◇◇◇◇◇◇◇◇◇◇◇◇◇◇◇◇◇

NAME OF
DESIGN:

CANVAS SIZE: _____

PICTURE SIZE: _____

SQUARE DRILL ☐   ROUND DRILL ○

I PURCHASED THIS KIT FROM:
(OR IT WAS GIFTED BY)

_____

PRICE: [   ]

DATE STARTED: / / /

DATE OF
COMPLETION: / / /

ADVANCED

INTERMEDIATE

BEGINNER

HOW MUCH I LOVED
THIS PROJECT ♡

◇ ◇ ◇ ◇ ◇

AFTER THE COMPLETION OF THIS PIECE I:

KEPT IT FOR MYSELF ◇   SOLD IT ◇

GIFTED IT TO A LOVED ONE ◇   OTHER ◇

I GIFTED IT TO: _____

OR I SOLD IT FOR [   ] ON/AT _____

_____ ON THE / / /

NOTES & IDEAS FOR THE NEXT PROJECT:

_____
_____
_____
_____

stick picture here

◇·◇·◇·◇·◇·◇·◇·◇·◇·◇·◇·◇·◇·◇·◇·◇·◇

NAME OF
DESIGN:

CANVAS SIZE: _____

PICTURE SIZE: _____

SQUARE DRILL ☐   ROUND DRILL ○

I PURCHASED THIS KIT FROM:
(OR IT WAS GIFTED BY)

_____

PRICE: [_____]

ADVANCED
_____
INTERMEDIATE
_____
BEGINNER

DATE STARTED: / / /

DATE OF
COMPLETION: / / /

HOW MUCH I LOVED
THIS PROJECT ♡

◇ ◇ ◇ ◇ ◇

AFTER THE COMPLETION OF THIS PIECE I:

KEPT IT FOR MYSELF ◇   SOLD IT ◇

GIFTED IT TO A LOVED ONE ◇   OTHER ◇

I GIFTED IT TO: _____

OR I SOLD IT FOR [_____] ON/AT _____

_____   ON THE / / /

NOTES & IDEAS FOR THE NEXT PROJECT:

_____

_____

_____

_____

_____

stick picture here

◇·◇·◇·◇·◇·◇·◇·◇·◇·◇·◇·◇·◇·◇·◇·◇·◇·◇

NAME OF
DESIGN:

CANVAS SIZE: _____

PICTURE SIZE: _____

SQUARE DRILL ☐   ROUND DRILL ○

DATE STARTED: / / /

DATE OF
COMPLETION: / / /

I PURCHASED THIS KIT FROM:
(OR IT WAS GIFTED BY)

ADVANCED

INTERMEDIATE

BEGINNER

_____

PRICE: [_____]

HOW MUCH I LOVED
THIS PROJECT ♡

◇ ◇ ◇ ◇ ◇

AFTER THE COMPLETION OF THIS PIECE I:

KEPT IT FOR MYSELF ◇   SOLD IT ◇

GIFTED IT TO A LOVED ONE ◇   OTHER ◇

I GIFTED IT TO: _____
OR I SOLD IT FOR [_____] ON/AT _____
_____ ON THE / / /

NOTES & IDEAS FOR THE NEXT PROJECT:

_____
_____
_____
_____

◇·◇·◇·◇·◇·◇·◇·◇·◇·◇·◇·◇·◇·◇·◇·◇·◇

stick picture here

NAME OF
DESIGN:

CANVAS SIZE: _____

PICTURE SIZE: _____

SQUARE DRILL ☐   ROUND DRILL ○

DATE STARTED: / / /

DATE OF
COMPLETION: / / /

ADVANCED
INTERMEDIATE
BEGINNER

I PURCHASED THIS KIT FROM:
(OR IT WAS GIFTED BY)

_____

PRICE: [   ]

HOW MUCH I LOVED
THIS PROJECT ♡

◇ ◇ ◇ ◇ ◇

AFTER THE COMPLETION OF THIS PIECE I:

KEPT IT FOR MYSELF ◇   SOLD IT ◇

GIFTED IT TO A LOVED ONE ◇   OTHER ◇

I GIFTED IT TO:_____

OR I SOLD IT FOR [   ] ON/AT

_____ ON THE / / /

NOTES & IDEAS FOR THE NEXT PROJECT:

_____

_____

_____

_____

stick picture here

◇•◇•◇•◇•◇•◇•◇•◇•◇•◇•◇•◇•◇•◇•◇

NAME OF
DESIGN:

CANVAS SIZE: _____
PICTURE SIZE: _____
SQUARE DRILL ☐   ROUND DRILL ○

DATE STARTED: / / /
DATE OF
COMPLETION: / / /

I PURCHASED THIS KIT FROM:
(OR IT WAS GIFTED BY)

ADVANCED
INTERMEDIATE
BEGINNER

HOW MUCH I LOVED
THIS PROJECT ♡
◇ ◇ ◇ ◇ ◇

_____

PRICE: [   ]

AFTER THE COMPLETION OF THIS PIECE I:

KEPT IT FOR MYSELF ◇   SOLD IT ◇

GIFTED IT TO A LOVED ONE ◇   OTHER ◇

I GIFTED IT TO:_____
OR I SOLD IT FOR [   ] ON/AT_____
_____ ON THE / / /

NOTES & IDEAS FOR THE NEXT PROJECT:

_____
_____
_____
_____

stick picture here

◇·◇·◇·◇·◇·◇·◇·◇·◇·◇·◇·◇·◇·◇·◇·◇·◇·◇·◇·◇

NAME OF DESIGN:

CANVAS SIZE: _____

PICTURE SIZE: _____

SQUARE DRILL ☐   ROUND DRILL ○

I PURCHASED THIS KIT FROM:
(OR IT WAS GIFTED BY)

_____

PRICE: [   ]

DATE STARTED: / / /

DATE OF
COMPLETION: / / /

ADVANCED
INTERMEDIATE
BEGINNER

HOW MUCH I LOVED
THIS PROJECT ♡

◇ ◇ ◇ ◇ ◇

AFTER THE COMPLETION OF THIS PIECE I:

KEPT IT FOR MYSELF ◇   SOLD IT ◇

GIFTED IT TO A LOVED ONE ◇   OTHER ◇

I GIFTED IT TO: _____

OR I SOLD IT FOR [   ] ON/AT

_____

ON THE / / /

NOTES & IDEAS FOR THE NEXT PROJECT:

_____

_____

_____

_____

stick picture here

◇·◇·◇·◇·◇·◇·◇·◇·◇·◇·◇·◇·◇·◇·◇·◇·◇·◇

NAME OF
DESIGN:

CANVAS SIZE: _____

PICTURE SIZE: _____

SQUARE DRILL ☐   ROUND DRILL ○

I PURCHASED THIS KIT FROM:
(OR IT WAS GIFTED BY)

_____

PRICE: [   ]

DATE STARTED: / / /

DATE OF
COMPLETION: / / /

ADVANCED
INTERMEDIATE
BEGINNER

HOW MUCH I LOVED
THIS PROJECT ♡
◇ ◇ ◇ ◇ ◇

AFTER THE COMPLETION OF THIS PIECE I:

KEPT IT FOR MYSELF ◇   SOLD IT ◇

GIFTED IT TO A LOVED ONE ◇   OTHER ◇

I GIFTED IT TO:_____
OR I SOLD IT FOR [   ] ON/AT_____
_____ ON THE / / /

NOTES & IDEAS FOR THE NEXT PROJECT:

_____
_____
_____
_____
_____

◇◇◇◇◇◇◇◇◇◇◇◇◇◇◇◇◇◇◇

stick picture here

NAME OF
DESIGN:

CANVAS SIZE: _____

PICTURE SIZE: _____

SQUARE DRILL ☐   ROUND DRILL ○

DATE STARTED: / / /
DATE OF
COMPLETION: / / /

I PURCHASED THIS KIT FROM:
(OR IT WAS GIFTED BY)

_____

PRICE: [   ]

ADVANCED
Intermediate
Beginner

HOW MUCH I LOVED
THIS PROJECT ♡

◇ ◇ ◇ ◇ ◇

AFTER THE COMPLETION OF THIS PIECE I:

KEPT IT FOR MYSELF ◇   SOLD IT ◇

GIFTED IT TO A LOVED ONE ◇   OTHER ◇

I GIFTED IT TO: _____
OR I SOLD IT FOR [   ] ON/AT _____
_____ ON THE / / /

NOTES & IDEAS FOR THE NEXT PROJECT:

_____
_____
_____
_____
_____

stick picture here

◇◇◇◇◇◇◇◇◇◇◇◇◇◇◇◇◇◇◇◇◇

NAME OF
DESIGN:

CANVAS SIZE: _____

PICTURE SIZE: _____

SQUARE DRILL ☐   ROUND DRILL ○

DATE STARTED: / / /

DATE OF
COMPLETION: / / /

I PURCHASED THIS KIT FROM:
(OR IT WAS GIFTED BY)

ADVANCED

INTERMEDIATE

BEGINNER

HOW MUCH I LOVED
THIS PROJECT ♡

◇ ◇ ◇ ◇ ◇

_____

PRICE: [   ]

AFTER THE COMPLETION OF THIS PIECE I:

KEPT IT FOR MYSELF ◇   SOLD IT ◇

GIFTED IT TO A LOVED ONE ◇   OTHER ◇

I GIFTED IT TO: _____

OR I SOLD IT FOR [   ] ON/AT _____

_____ ON THE / / /

NOTES & IDEAS FOR THE NEXT PROJECT:

_____
_____
_____
_____
_____

stick picture here

◇·◇·◇·◇·◇·◇·◇·◇·◇·◇·◇·◇·◇·◇·◇·◇·◇·◇

NAME OF
DESIGN:

CANVAS SIZE: _____

PICTURE SIZE: _____

SQUARE DRILL ☐   ROUND DRILL ○

I PURCHASED THIS KIT FROM:
(OR IT WAS GIFTED BY)

_____

PRICE: [   ]

AFTER THE COMPLETION OF THIS PIECE I:

KEPT IT FOR MYSELF ◇   SOLD IT ◇

GIFTED IT TO A LOVED ONE ◇   OTHER ◇

I GIFTED IT TO:_____
OR I SOLD IT FOR [   ] ON/AT_____
_____ ON THE / /

NOTES & IDEAS FOR THE NEXT PROJECT:

_____
_____
_____
_____
_____

DATE STARTED: / /
DATE OF
COMPLETION: / /

ADVANCED
INTERMEDIATE
BEGINNER

HOW MUCH I LOVED
THIS PROJECT ♡

◇ ◇ ◇ ◇ ◇

stick picture here

◇·◇·◇·◇·◇·◇·◇·◇·◇·◇·◇·◇·◇·◇·◇·◇·◇·◇

NAME OF
DESIGN:

CANVAS SIZE: _____

PICTURE SIZE: _____

SQUARE DRILL ☐   ROUND DRILL ○

I PURCHASED THIS KIT FROM:
(OR IT WAS GIFTED BY)

_____

PRICE: [＿＿＿]

DATE STARTED: / / /

DATE OF
COMPLETION: / / /

ADVANCED

INTERMEDIATE

BEGINNER

HOW MUCH I LOVED
THIS PROJECT ♡

◇ ◇ ◇ ◇ ◇

AFTER THE COMPLETION OF THIS PIECE I:

KEPT IT FOR MYSELF ◇   SOLD IT ◇

GIFTED IT TO A LOVED ONE ◇   OTHER ◇

I GIFTED IT TO: _____

OR I SOLD IT FOR [＿＿＿] ON/AT _____

_____ ON THE / / /

NOTES & IDEAS FOR THE NEXT PROJECT:

_____

_____

_____

_____

◇·◇·◇·◇·◇·◇·◇·◇·◇·◇·◇·◇·◇·◇·◇·◇·◇

stick picture here

NAME OF
DESIGN:

CANVAS SIZE: _____

PICTURE SIZE: _____

SQUARE DRILL ☐   ROUND DRILL ◯

DATE STARTED: / / /
DATE OF
COMPLETION: / / /

I PURCHASED THIS KIT FROM:
(OR IT WAS GIFTED BY)

ADVANCED

INTERMEDIATE

BEGINNER

HOW MUCH I LOVED
THIS PROJECT ♡
◇ ◇ ◇ ◇ ◇

_____

PRICE: [_____]

AFTER THE COMPLETION OF THIS PIECE I:

KEPT IT FOR MYSELF ◇   SOLD IT ◇

GIFTED IT TO A LOVED ONE ◇   OTHER ◇

I GIFTED IT TO:_____
OR I SOLD IT FOR [_____] ON/AT_____
_____ ON THE / / /

NOTES & IDEAS FOR THE NEXT PROJECT:

_____

_____

_____

_____

_____

stick picture here

◇◇◇◇◇◇◇◇◇◇◇◇◇◇◇◇◇◇◇◇◇

NAME OF
DESIGN:

CANVAS SIZE: _____

PICTURE SIZE: _____

SQUARE DRILL ☐   ROUND DRILL ○

I PURCHASED THIS KIT FROM:
(OR IT WAS GIFTED BY)

_____

PRICE: [_____]

DATE STARTED: / / /

DATE OF
COMPLETION: / / /

ADVANCED
INTERMEDIATE
BEGINNER

HOW MUCH I LOVED
THIS PROJECT ♡

◇ ◇ ◇ ◇ ◇

AFTER THE COMPLETION OF THIS PIECE I:

KEPT IT FOR MYSELF ◇   SOLD IT ◇

GIFTED IT TO A LOVED ONE ◇   OTHER ◇

I GIFTED IT TO:_____

OR I SOLD IT FOR [_____] ON/AT _____

_____ ON THE / / /

NOTES & IDEAS FOR THE NEXT PROJECT:

_____

_____

_____

_____

_____

◇•◇•◇•◇•◇•◇•◇•◇•◇•◇•◇•◇•◇•◇•◇•◇

stick picture here

NAME OF
DESIGN:

CANVAS SIZE: _____

PICTURE SIZE: _____

SQUARE DRILL ☐   ROUND DRILL ○

DATE STARTED: / / /

DATE OF
COMPLETION: / / /

I PURCHASED THIS KIT FROM:
(OR IT WAS GIFTED BY)

ADVANCED
INTERMEDIATE
BEGINNER

HOW MUCH I LOVED
THIS PROJECT ♡

◇ ◇ ◇ ◇ ◇

_____

PRICE: [_____]

AFTER THE COMPLETION OF THIS PIECE I:

KEPT IT FOR MYSELF ◇   SOLD IT ◇

GIFTED IT TO A LOVED ONE ◇   OTHER ◇

I GIFTED IT TO: _____

OR I SOLD IT FOR [_____] ON/AT _____

_____ ON THE / / /

NOTES & IDEAS FOR THE NEXT PROJECT:

_____

_____

_____

_____

_____

STICK PICTURE HERE

◇◇◇◇ ◇◇◇ ◇◇◇◇ ◇◇◇◇◇◇◇◇◇◇◇

NAME OF
DESIGN:

CANVAS SIZE: _____

PICTURE SIZE: _____

SQUARE DRILL ☐   ROUND DRILL ○

I PURCHASED THIS KIT FROM:
(OR IT WAS GIFTED BY)

_____

PRICE: [   ]

ADVANCED

INTERMEDIATE

BEGINNER

DATE STARTED: / / /

DATE OF
COMPLETION: / / /

HOW MUCH I LOVED
THIS PROJECT ♡

◇ ◇ ◇ ◇ ◇

AFTER THE COMPLETION OF THIS PIECE I:

KEPT IT FOR MYSELF ◇   SOLD IT ◇

GIFTED IT TO A LOVED ONE ◇   OTHER ◇

I GIFTED IT TO: _____

OR I SOLD IT FOR [   ] ON/AT _____

_____ ON THE / / /

NOTES & IDEAS FOR THE NEXT PROJECT:

_____

_____

_____

_____

_____

◇◇◇◇◇◇◇◇◇◇◇◇◇◇◇◇◇◇◇

stick picture here

NAME OF
DESIGN:

CANVAS SIZE: _____

PICTURE SIZE: _____

SQUARE DRILL ☐   ROUND DRILL ○

I PURCHASED THIS KIT FROM:
(OR IT WAS GIFTED BY)

_____

PRICE: [_____]

DATE STARTED: / /

DATE OF
COMPLETION: / /

ADVANCED

INTERMEDIATE

BEGINNER

HOW MUCH I LOVED
THIS PROJECT ♡

◇ ◇ ◇ ◇ ◇

AFTER THE COMPLETION OF THIS PIECE I:

KEPT IT FOR MYSELF ◇   SOLD IT ◇

GIFTED IT TO A LOVED ONE ◇   OTHER ◇

I GIFTED IT TO: _____

OR I SOLD IT FOR [_____] ON/AT

_____ ON THE / /

NOTES & IDEAS FOR THE NEXT PROJECT:

_____

_____

_____

_____

_____

stick picture here

◇◇◇◇◇◇◇◇◇◇◇◇◇◇◇◇◇◇◇◇◇◇

NAME OF
DESIGN:

CANVAS SIZE: _____

PICTURE SIZE: _____

SQUARE DRILL ☐   ROUND DRILL ○

I PURCHASED THIS KIT FROM:
(OR IT WAS GIFTED BY)

_____

PRICE: [   ]

DATE STARTED: / / /
DATE OF
COMPLETION: / / /

ADVANCED
INTERMEDIATE
BEGINNER

HOW MUCH I LOVED
THIS PROJECT ♡

◇ ◇ ◇ ◇ ◇

AFTER THE COMPLETION OF THIS PIECE I:

KEPT IT FOR MYSELF ◇   SOLD IT ◇

GIFTED IT TO A LOVED ONE ◇   OTHER ◇

I GIFTED IT TO:_____

OR I SOLD IT FOR [   ] ON/AT _____

ON THE / / /

NOTES & IDEAS FOR THE NEXT PROJECT:

_____

_____

_____

_____

◇·◇·◇·◇·◇·◇·◇·◇·◇·◇·◇·◇·◇·◇·◇·◇·◇·◇·◇·◇

stick picture here

NAME OF
DESIGN:

CANVAS SIZE: _____

PICTURE SIZE: _____

SQUARE DRILL ☐   ROUND DRILL ○

I PURCHASED THIS KIT FROM:
(OR IT WAS GIFTED BY)

_____

PRICE: [   ]

DATE STARTED: / / /

DATE OF
COMPLETION: / / /

ADVANCED
INTERMEDIATE
BEGINNER

HOW MUCH I LOVED
THIS PROJECT ♡

◇ ◇ ◇ ◇ ◇

AFTER THE COMPLETION OF THIS PIECE I:

KEPT IT FOR MYSELF ◇   SOLD IT ◇

GIFTED IT TO A LOVED ONE ◇   OTHER ◇

I GIFTED IT TO: _____

OR I SOLD IT FOR [   ] ON/AT _____

_____ ON THE / / /

NOTES & IDEAS FOR THE NEXT PROJECT:

_____

_____

_____

_____

_____

stick picture here

◇◇◇◇◇◇◇◇◇◇◇◇◇◇◇◇◇◇◇◇◇◇

NAME OF
DESIGN:

CANVAS SIZE: _____

PICTURE SIZE: _____

SQUARE DRILL ☐   ROUND DRILL ○

I PURCHASED THIS KIT FROM:
(OR IT WAS GIFTED BY)

_____

PRICE: [   ]

AFTER THE COMPLETION OF THIS PIECE I:

KEPT IT FOR MYSELF ◇   SOLD IT ◇

GIFTED IT TO A LOVED ONE ◇   OTHER ◇

I GIFTED IT TO: _____

OR I SOLD IT FOR [   ] ON/AT _____

_____ ON THE / /

NOTES & IDEAS FOR THE NEXT PROJECT:

_____
_____
_____
_____
_____

◇·◇·◇·◇·◇·◇·◇·◇·◇·◇·◇·◇·◇·◇·◇·◇·◇·◇

DATE STARTED: / /

DATE OF
COMPLETION: / /

ADVANCED

INTERMEDIATE

BEGINNER

HOW MUCH I LOVED
THIS PROJECT ♥

◇ ◇ ◇ ◇ ◇

stick picture here

NAME OF
DESIGN:

CANVAS SIZE: _____

PICTURE SIZE: _____

SQUARE DRILL ☐   ROUND DRILL ○

DATE STARTED: / / /

DATE OF
COMPLETION: / / /

I PURCHASED THIS KIT FROM:
(OR IT WAS GIFTED BY)

ADVANCED

INTERMEDIATE

BEGINNER

HOW MUCH I LOVED
THIS PROJECT ♡

◇ ◇ ◇ ◇ ◇

_____

PRICE: [   ]

AFTER THE COMPLETION OF THIS PIECE I:

KEPT IT FOR MYSELF ◇   SOLD IT ◇

GIFTED IT TO A LOVED ONE ◇   OTHER ◇

I GIFTED IT TO: _____

OR I SOLD IT FOR [   ] ON/AT _____

_____ ON THE / / /

NOTES & IDEAS FOR THE NEXT PROJECT:

_____

_____

_____

_____

stick picture here

◇·◇·◇·◇·◇·◇·◇·◇·◇·◇·◇·◇·◇·◇·◇·◇·◇·◇·◇

NAME OF
DESIGN:

CANVAS SIZE: _____

PICTURE SIZE: _____

SQUARE DRILL ☐   ROUND DRILL ○

DATE STARTED: / / /

DATE OF
COMPLETION: / / /

I PURCHASED THIS KIT FROM:
(OR IT WAS GIFTED BY)

ADVANCED

INTERMEDIATE

BEGINNER

HOW MUCH I LOVED
THIS PROJECT ♡

◇ ◇ ◇ ◇ ◇

_____

PRICE: [   ]

AFTER THE COMPLETION OF THIS PIECE I:

KEPT IT FOR MYSELF ◇   SOLD IT ◇

GIFTED IT TO A LOVED ONE ◇   OTHER ◇

I GIFTED IT TO: _____

OR I SOLD IT FOR [   ] ON/AT _____

_____ ON THE / / /

NOTES & IDEAS FOR THE NEXT PROJECT:

_____

_____

_____

_____

stick picture here

◇·◇·◇·◇·◇·◇·◇·◇·◇·◇·◇·◇·◇·◇·◇·◇

NAME OF
DESIGN:

CANVAS SIZE: _____

PICTURE SIZE: _____

SQUARE DRILL ☐   ROUND DRILL ◯

I PURCHASED THIS KIT FROM:
(OR IT WAS GIFTED BY)

_____

PRICE: [＿＿＿＿]

DATE STARTED: / / /

DATE OF
COMPLETION: / / /

ADVANCED
INTERMEDIATE
BEGINNER

HOW MUCH I LOVED
THIS PROJECT ♡

◇ ◇ ◇ ◇ ◇

AFTER THE COMPLETION OF THIS PIECE I:

KEPT IT FOR MYSELF ◇   SOLD IT ◇

GIFTED IT TO A LOVED ONE ◇   OTHER ◇

I GIFTED IT TO:_____
OR I SOLD IT FOR [＿＿＿] ON/AT_____
_____ ON THE / / /

NOTES & IDEAS FOR THE NEXT PROJECT:
_____
_____
_____
_____

stick picture here

◇·◇·◇·◇·◇·◇·◇·◇·◇·◇·◇·◇·◇·◇·◇·◇·◇·◇·◇

NAME OF
DESIGN:

CANVAS SIZE: _____

PICTURE SIZE: _____

SQUARE DRILL ☐   ROUND DRILL ○

DATE STARTED: / / /

DATE OF
COMPLETION: / / /

ADVANCED
INTERMEDIATE
BEGINNER

I PURCHASED THIS KIT FROM:
(OR IT WAS GIFTED BY)

_____

PRICE: [_____]

HOW MUCH I LOVED
THIS PROJECT ♡

◇ ◇ ◇ ◇ ◇

AFTER THE COMPLETION OF THIS PIECE I:

KEPT IT FOR MYSELF ◇   SOLD IT ◇

GIFTED IT TO A LOVED ONE ◇   OTHER ◇

I GIFTED IT TO: _____

OR I SOLD IT FOR [_____] ON/AT _____

_____ ON THE / / /

NOTES & IDEAS FOR THE NEXT PROJECT:

_____
_____
_____
_____

stick picture here

◇·◇·◇·◇·◇·◇·◇·◇·◇·◇·◇·◇·◇·◇·◇·◇·◇·◇·◇◇·◇

NAME OF
DESIGN:

CANVAS SIZE: _____

PICTURE SIZE: _____

SQUARE DRILL ☐   ROUND DRILL ○

DATE STARTED: / / /

DATE OF
COMPLETION: / / /

I PURCHASED THIS KIT FROM:
(OR IT WAS GIFTED BY)

ADVANCED

INTERMEDIATE

BEGINNER

HOW MUCH I LOVED
THIS PROJECT ♡

◇ ◇ ◇ ◇ ◇

_____

PRICE: [   ]

AFTER THE COMPLETION OF THIS PIECE I:

KEPT IT FOR MYSELF ◇   SOLD IT ◇

GIFTED IT TO A LOVED ONE ◇   OTHER ◇

I GIFTED IT TO: _____

OR I SOLD IT FOR [   ] ON/AT _____

_____ ON THE / / /

NOTES & IDEAS FOR THE NEXT PROJECT:

_____

_____

_____

_____

stick picture here

◇◇◇◇◇◇◇◇◇◇◇◇◇◇◇◇◇◇◇◇◇◇◇

NAME OF
DESIGN:

CANVAS SIZE: _____

PICTURE SIZE: _____

SQUARE DRILL ☐   ROUND DRILL ○

I PURCHASED THIS KIT FROM:
(OR IT WAS GIFTED BY)

_____

PRICE: [   ]

ADVANCED
Intermediate
Beginner

DATE STARTED: / / /
DATE OF
COMPLETION: / / /

HOW MUCH I LOVED
THIS PROJECT ♡

◇ ◇ ◇ ◇ ◇

AFTER THE COMPLETION OF THIS PIECE I:

KEPT IT FOR MYSELF ◇   SOLD IT ◇

GIFTED IT TO A LOVED ONE ◇   OTHER ◇

I GIFTED IT TO: _____
OR I SOLD IT FOR [   ] ON/AT _____
_____ ON THE / / /

NOTES & IDEAS FOR THE NEXT PROJECT:

_____
_____
_____
_____

◇·◇·◇·◇·◇·◇·◇·◇·◇·◇·◇·◇·◇·◇·◇

stick picture here

NAME OF
DESIGN:

CANVAS SIZE: _____

PICTURE SIZE: _____

SQUARE DRILL ☐   ROUND DRILL ◯

DATE STARTED: / / /

DATE OF
COMPLETION: / / /

I PURCHASED THIS KIT FROM:
(OR IT WAS GIFTED BY)

ADVANCED

INTERMEDIATE

BEGINNER

HOW MUCH I LOVED
THIS PROJECT ♡

◇ ◇ ◇ ◇ ◇

_____

PRICE: [   ]

AFTER THE COMPLETION OF THIS PIECE I:

KEPT IT FOR MYSELF ◇   SOLD IT ◇

GIFTED IT TO A LOVED ONE ◇   OTHER ◇

I GIFTED IT TO:_____

OR I SOLD IT FOR [   ] ON/AT _____

_____ ON THE / / /

NOTES & IDEAS FOR THE NEXT PROJECT:

_____

_____

_____

_____

_____

stick picture here

◇◇◇◇◇◇◇◇◇◇◇◇◇◇◇◇◇◇◇◇◇◇◇◇

NAME OF
DESIGN:

CANVAS SIZE: _____

PICTURE SIZE: _____

SQUARE DRILL ☐   ROUND DRILL ○

I PURCHASED THIS KIT FROM:
(OR IT WAS GIFTED BY)

ADVANCED
INTERMEDIATE
BEGINNER

_____

PRICE: [   ]

AFTER THE COMPLETION OF THIS PIECE I:

KEPT IT FOR MYSELF ◇   SOLD IT ◇

GIFTED IT TO A LOVED ONE ◇   OTHER ◇

I GIFTED IT TO: _____
OR I SOLD IT FOR [   ] ON/AT _____

_____ ON THE / / /

NOTES & IDEAS FOR THE NEXT PROJECT:

_____

_____

_____

_____

DATE STARTED: / / /

DATE OF
COMPLETION: / / /

HOW MUCH I LOVED
THIS PROJECT ♡

◇ ◇ ◇ ◇ ◇

stick picture here

◇·◇·◇·◇·◇·◇·◇·◇·◇·◇·◇·◇·◇·◇·◇·◇·◇·◇

NAME OF DESIGN:

CANVAS SIZE: _____

PICTURE SIZE: _____

SQUARE DRILL ☐   ROUND DRILL ○

I PURCHASED THIS KIT FROM:
(OR IT WAS GIFTED BY)

_____

PRICE: [_____]

DATE STARTED: / / /

DATE OF
COMPLETION: / / /

ADVANCED
Intermediate
Beginner

HOW MUCH I LOVED
THIS PROJECT ♡

◇ ◇ ◇ ◇ ◇

AFTER THE COMPLETION OF THIS PIECE I:

KEPT IT FOR MYSELF ◇   SOLD IT ◇

GIFTED IT TO A LOVED ONE ◇   OTHER ◇

I GIFTED IT TO: _____

OR I SOLD IT FOR [_____] ON/AT _____

_____ ON THE / / /

NOTES & IDEAS FOR THE NEXT PROJECT:

_____

_____

_____

_____

_____

◇•◇•◇•◇•◇•◇•◇•◇•◇•◇•◇•◇•◇•◇•◇•◇•◇

stick picture here

NAME OF
DESIGN:

CANVAS SIZE: _____

PICTURE SIZE: _____

SQUARE DRILL ☐   ROUND DRILL ○

DATE STARTED: / / /

DATE OF
COMPLETION: / / /

I PURCHASED THIS KIT FROM:
(OR IT WAS GIFTED BY)

ADVANCED

INTERMEDIATE

BEGINNER

HOW MUCH I LOVED
THIS PROJECT ♡

◇ ◇ ◇ ◇ ◇

_____

PRICE: [   ]

AFTER THE COMPLETION OF THIS PIECE I:

KEPT IT FOR MYSELF ◇ SOLD IT ◇

GIFTED IT TO A LOVED ONE ◇ OTHER ◇

I GIFTED IT TO: _____

OR I SOLD IT FOR [   ] ON/AT _____

_____ ON THE / / /

NOTES & IDEAS FOR THE NEXT PROJECT:

_____

_____

_____

_____

◇◇◇◇◇◇◇◇◇◇◇◇◇◇◇◇◇◇◇

stick picture here

NAME OF
DESIGN:

CANVAS SIZE: _____

PICTURE SIZE: _____

SQUARE DRILL ☐   ROUND DRILL ◯

DATE STARTED: / / /

DATE OF
COMPLETION: / / /

I PURCHASED THIS KIT FROM:
(OR IT WAS GIFTED BY)

ADVANCED

INTERMEDIATE

BEGINNER

HOW MUCH I LOVED
THIS PROJECT ♡

◇ ◇ ◇ ◇ ◇

_____

PRICE: [   ]

AFTER THE COMPLETION OF THIS PIECE I:

KEPT IT FOR MYSELF ◇   SOLD IT ◇

GIFTED IT TO A LOVED ONE ◇   OTHER ◇

I GIFTED IT TO: _____

OR I SOLD IT FOR [   ] ON/AT _____

_____ ON THE / / /

NOTES & IDEAS FOR THE NEXT PROJECT:

_____

_____

_____

_____

stick picture here

◇•◇•◇•◇•◇•◇•◇•◇•◇•◇•◇•◇•◇•◇•◇•◇•◇•◇

NAME OF
DESIGN:

CANVAS SIZE: _____

PICTURE SIZE: _____

SQUARE DRILL ☐   ROUND DRILL ○

DATE STARTED: / / /

DATE OF
COMPLETION: / / /

I PURCHASED THIS KIT FROM:
(OR IT WAS GIFTED BY)

ADVANCED
INTERMEDIATE
BEGINNER

HOW MUCH I LOVED
THIS PROJECT ♡

◇ ◇ ◇ ◇ ◇

_____

PRICE: [   ]

AFTER THE COMPLETION OF THIS PIECE I:

KEPT IT FOR MYSELF ◇   SOLD IT ◇

GIFTED IT TO A LOVED ONE ◇   OTHER ◇

I GIFTED IT TO: _____

OR I SOLD IT FOR [   ] ON/AT _____

_____ ON THE / / /

NOTES & IDEAS FOR THE NEXT PROJECT:

_____

_____

_____

_____

◇◇◇◇◇◇◇◇◇◇◇◇◇◇◇◇◇◇◇◇◇◇◇

stick picture here

NAME OF
DESIGN:

CANVAS SIZE: _____

PICTURE SIZE: _____

SQUARE DRILL ☐   ROUND DRILL ○

DATE STARTED: / / /

DATE OF
COMPLETION: / / /

I PURCHASED THIS KIT FROM:
(OR IT WAS GIFTED BY)

_____

PRICE: [   ]

ADVANCED

INTERMEDIATE

BEGINNER

HOW MUCH I LOVED
THIS PROJECT ♡

◇ ◇ ◇ ◇ ◇

AFTER THE COMPLETION OF THIS PIECE I:

KEPT IT FOR MYSELF ◇   SOLD IT ◇

GIFTED IT TO A LOVED ONE ◇   OTHER ◇

I GIFTED IT TO:_____
OR I SOLD IT FOR [   ] ON/AT_____
_____ ON THE / / /

NOTES & IDEAS FOR THE NEXT PROJECT:

_____
_____
_____
_____
_____

◇◇◇◇◇◇◇◇◇◇◇◇◇◇◇◇◇◇◇◇

stick picture here

NAME OF
DESIGN:

CANVAS SIZE: _____

PICTURE SIZE: _____

SQUARE DRILL ☐   ROUND DRILL ○

I PURCHASED THIS KIT FROM:
(OR IT WAS GIFTED BY)

_____

PRICE: [   ]

DATE STARTED: / / /

DATE OF
COMPLETION: / / /

ADVANCED
INTERMEDIATE
BEGINNER

HOW MUCH I LOVED
THIS PROJECT ♡

◇ ◇ ◇ ◇ ◇

AFTER THE COMPLETION OF THIS PIECE I:

KEPT IT FOR MYSELF ◇   SOLD IT ◇

GIFTED IT TO A LOVED ONE ◇   OTHER ◇

I GIFTED IT TO: _____

OR I SOLD IT FOR [   ] ON/AT _____

_____ ON THE / / /

NOTES & IDEAS FOR THE NEXT PROJECT:

_____

_____

_____

_____

◇•◇•◇•◇•◇•◇•◇•◇•◇•◇•◇•◇•◇•◇•◇

stick picture here

NAME OF
DESIGN:

CANVAS SIZE: _____

PICTURE SIZE: _____

SQUARE DRILL ☐   ROUND DRILL ○

I PURCHASED THIS KIT FROM:
(OR IT WAS GIFTED BY)

_____

PRICE: [ ]

ADVANCED

INTERMEDIATE

BEGINNER

DATE STARTED: / / /

DATE OF
COMPLETION: / / /

HOW MUCH I LOVED
THIS PROJECT ♡

◇ ◇ ◇ ◇ ◇

AFTER THE COMPLETION OF THIS PIECE I:

KEPT IT FOR MYSELF ◇   SOLD IT ◇

GIFTED IT TO A LOVED ONE ◇   OTHER ◇

I GIFTED IT TO:_____
OR I SOLD IT FOR [ ] ON/AT_____

_____ ON THE / / /

NOTES & IDEAS FOR THE NEXT PROJECT:

_____

_____

_____

_____

_____

_____

stick picture here

◇◇◇◇◇◇◇◇◇◇◇◇◇◇◇◇◇◇◇◇◇◇◇◇

NAME OF
DESIGN:

CANVAS SIZE: _____

PICTURE SIZE: _____

SQUARE DRILL ☐   ROUND DRILL ○

I PURCHASED THIS KIT FROM:
(OR IT WAS GIFTED BY)

_____

PRICE: [_____]

AFTER THE COMPLETION OF THIS PIECE I:

KEPT IT FOR MYSELF ◇   SOLD IT ◇

GIFTED IT TO A LOVED ONE ◇   OTHER ◇

I GIFTED IT TO: _____

OR I SOLD IT FOR [_____] ON/AT _____

_____ ON THE / / /

NOTES & IDEAS FOR THE NEXT PROJECT:

_____
_____
_____
_____
_____

◇·◇·◇·◇·◇·◇·◇·◇·◇·◇·◇·◇·◇·◇·◇·◇·◇

DATE STARTED: / / /

DATE OF
COMPLETION: / / /

ADVANCED
INTERMEDIATE
BEGINNER

HOW MUCH I LOVED
THIS PROJECT ♡

◇ ◇ ◇ ◇ ◇

stick picture here

NAME OF
DESIGN:

CANVAS SIZE: _____

PICTURE SIZE: _____

SQUARE DRILL ☐   ROUND DRILL ○

DATE STARTED: / / /

DATE OF
COMPLETION: / / /

I PURCHASED THIS KIT FROM:
(OR IT WAS GIFTED BY)

ADVANCED

INTERMEDIATE

BEGINNER

HOW MUCH I LOVED
THIS PROJECT ♡

◇ ◇ ◇ ◇ ◇

PRICE: [_____]

AFTER THE COMPLETION OF THIS PIECE I:

KEPT IT FOR MYSELF ◇   SOLD IT ◇

GIFTED IT TO A LOVED ONE ◇   OTHER ◇

I GIFTED IT TO: _____

OR I SOLD IT FOR [_____] ON/AT _____

_____ ON THE / / /

NOTES & IDEAS FOR THE NEXT PROJECT:

_____

_____

_____

_____

_____

stick picture here

◇◇◇◇◇◇◇◇◇◇◇◇◇◇◇◇◇◇◇

NAME OF
DESIGN:

CANVAS SIZE: _____

PICTURE SIZE: _____

SQUARE DRILL ☐   ROUND DRILL ○

DATE STARTED: / / /

DATE OF
COMPLETION: / / /

I PURCHASED THIS KIT FROM:
(OR IT WAS GIFTED BY)

ADVANCED
INTERMEDIATE
BEGINNER

HOW MUCH I LOVED
THIS PROJECT ♡

◇ ◇ ◇ ◇ ◇

_____

PRICE: ☐

AFTER THE COMPLETION OF THIS PIECE I:

KEPT IT FOR MYSELF ◇   SOLD IT ◇

GIFTED IT TO A LOVED ONE ◇   OTHER ◇

I GIFTED IT TO: _____

OR I SOLD IT FOR ☐ ON/AT

_____ ON THE / / /

NOTES & IDEAS FOR THE NEXT PROJECT:

_____

_____

_____

_____

◇·◇·◇·◇·◇·◇·◇·◇·◇·◇·◇·◇·◇·◇·◇·◇

stick picture here

Made in the USA
Las Vegas, NV
06 May 2022

48504404R00059